PUFFI.

THE WILD PACK DEVISES A PLAN

André Marx studied German language and literature, linguistics and art at the University of Osnabrück. He then became a full-time writer, authoring twenty-seven books of the German cult series 'Die Drei ???'. He is known for his witty wordplay and for masterfully weaving mysterious clues, thrills and suspense into his stories. In 2007, he collaborated with Boris Pfeiffer on the Wild Pack series for children.

Born in 1964 in Berlin, **Boris Pfeiffer** is a German writer of children's books, plays and poetry. He worked as a stage director and screenwriter before going on to become an author and award-winning playwright. His books have sold over a million copies in Germany, and his stories have been translated into nine languages.

Anya Malhotra has been a freelance translator and interpreter for close to twenty-five years. Her work spans a wide range, from literature and technical texts to environmental and economic research. Her translations have also been published in magazines and have appeared online. Anya's childhood was spent surrounded by books but, much to her regret, no animals, which she is making up for now. An outdoor person, she divides her time between Delhi and Kumaon.

Read More in the Series:

The Wild Pack

The Wild Pack
Devises a Plan

André Marx
Boris Pfeiffer

Illustrations by Sebastian Meyer

Translated from the German by Anya Malhotra

PUFFIN BOOKS
An imprint of Penguin Random House

PUFFIN BOOKS

USA | Canada | UK | Ireland | Australia
New Zealand | India | South Africa | China

Puffin Books is part of the Penguin Random House group of companies
whose addresses can be found at global.penguinrandomhouse.com

Published by Penguin Random House India Pvt. Ltd
7th Floor, Infinity Tower C, DLF Cyber City,
Gurgaon 122 002, Haryana, India

Penguin
Random House
India

First published in German as *Das Wilde Pack Schmiedet Einen Plan Band 2* by
Franckh-Kosmos Verlags-GmbH & Co.KG, Stuttgart 2007
Published in Puffin Books by Penguin Random House India 2017

10 9 8 7 6 5 4 3 2 1

ISBN 9780143334293

For sale in the Indian Subcontinent only

Typeset in Apollo MT by R. Ajith Kumar, New Delhi
Printed at Thomson Press India Ltd, New Delhi

www.penguin.co.in

To everyone who played a part,
I thank you with all my heart.
For my pack of friends a special thanks,
On them I can always bank.

—Anya Malhotra

GOETHE INSTITUT

The translation of this work is supported by a grant from the Goethe-Institut, which is funded by the German Ministry of Foreign Affairs.

Chapter 1

It was a perfectly ordinary day in the city.

Cars crawled through the streets past building sites, bicycle bells tringed and people hurried across the pavements with shopping bags. A group of school children laughed and played as they skipped home, while businessmen in dark suits stepped into posh restaurants in their lunch break.

In one such restaurant sat Mueller, the director of the city zoo, with his three daughters, Amanda, Babette and Constance. They were seated at a round table covered with a spotless white tablecloth, beneath a glittering chandelier. Soft violin music played in the background.

Amanda, the eldest, with flaming red hair, was busy rummaging through her crocodile-leather bag for a small mirror. She had to check on her lipstick every five minutes, otherwise she felt insecure and ugly. Babette, the middle daughter with straw blonde hair, had her nose buried in the menu. She couldn't make up her mind and was wavering between frog legs and snails. Lost in thought, she chewed on her fingers clad in zebra-skin gloves.

Only Constance, the youngest, showed no interest in either the menu or her appearance. She hardly noticed her father and sisters. Her gaze was fixed on the large package wrapped in shiny gift paper that her father had brought along and which now lay next to the table. She jiggled her feet restlessly.

'Go on now, Papa, give it to her,' muttered Babette, 'or we'll have no peace.'

Constance stuck her tongue out at her sister, but then her father bent down, picked up the present and handed it to her across the table. 'All right then. Happy sixteenth birthday, my poppet!'

Constance snatched the package greedily, not even bothering to look at her father. It was suspiciously light. A strand of her hair, black as car tyres, fell across her face. She brushed it away and tore at the paper. Then, heart beating fast, she lifted the lid.

A shimmering, ivory-coloured cloth slithered out, delicate and light as smoke. It was an evening dress of pure silk, embroidered with glistening pearls.

Constance clawed the dress. Furiously, she stared at her father.

Zoo Director Mueller swallowed hard. 'Don't you like it, darling?'

'A silk dress? Do I like it? You're asking me? I wanted a fur coat! A fur coat made of wolf fur!'

'Yes, I know, darling, but this is genuine Chinese silk! It's much more expensive than . . .'

'Do you think I care! Amanda and Babette also got fur coats on their sixteenth birthday! Polar bear and tiger! And I wanted wolf!'

'That's true, Papa,' said Amanda, finally managing to tear her gaze from the little mirror in her hand. 'That's not fair. Why hasn't Constance got a fur coat?'

'Yes!' shrieked Constance. 'Why haven't I got a fur coat?'

Zoo Director Mueller suddenly felt very hot in his black suit. He had suspected it would be a difficult situation, but *this* difficult? He dabbed his forehead with a handkerchief. 'Now listen, darling . . . I did want to gift you a wolf fur! But the wolf escaped from my zoo. You know that, you saw it yourself!'

'Yes, and you went after him, Papa, I saw that too!' spat Constance. 'So? What happened?'

Mueller swallowed again. 'I . . . well, I don't know how to explain, my precious. I followed the wolf through half the city, but then somehow . . . you know . . . I lost sight of him.'

That wasn't the entire truth. The truth was that Mueller had forgotten what had happened. He had followed the wolf . . . and the next thing he knew, he had woken up in his jeep at a scrapyard. What happened in between had strangely been erased from Mueller's memory. But he didn't want to tell his daughters that. After this incident, still rather woozy and confused, he had driven back to the zoo. And to top it all, the gorilla whose fur he had thought of gifting to Constance instead of the wolf had managed to get away too!

Ever since, Mueller felt as if he had a bad cold. His head seemed stuffed with cotton wool, his vision was fuzzy and once a day he would break out in a cold sweat. Sometimes weird images would flash through his head: images of underground passages and giant snakes. He hoped these were just strange dreams.

Constance was not interested in her father's explanations. She banged on the table so furiously that the glasses rattled. Some guests turned around and started whispering. But Constance didn't care. 'You are mean! You love Amanda and Babette much more than me!'

'But that's not true, my love! Just look, this silk is from China and . . .'

'I don't want your stupid silk! I want you to shoot a wild animal for me and make it into a fur coat like you did for Amanda and Babette. And I want a wolf!'

Babette finally looked up from the menu. Constance hoped that her sister would support her. But Babette only said, 'I think I know now. I'll take the frog legs *and* the snails!'

'Stupid cow!' screeched Constance and jumped up. Her father's glass of red wine toppled and the blood-red liquid spilled over the ivory silk. But Constance didn't give a fig about the stupid dress. Let her father realize that she wouldn't let herself be fobbed off so easily.

Furiously, she marched towards the exit, when all of a sudden it began to rain.

Not outside on the street but right inside the restaurant!

It was raining from the ceiling. Water sprayed from little nozzles and within seconds it had soaked the light-coloured carpet, the damask tablecloths, the wine-spattered silk dress along with the starters, main courses and desserts of the guests. And of course, the guests themselves.

People screamed and jumped up.

'Fire!' shouted someone. 'That is the fire alarm! Everyone out!'

At once, panic broke out. Women held their handbags over their heads and began to run. Men hid under their suit jackets and ran after them. A waiter dressed in black and white attempted to restore order but was simply trampled. The cooks in their grease-spattered aprons rushed out through the large swing doors, clutching their ladles. Everyone screamed and charged out through the spraying water.

A minute later the restaurant was empty. All the guests, waiters and cooks stood outside on the street, yelling in confusion. Zoo Director Mueller tried at first to calm his three daughters who were beside themselves with indignation. When that didn't work, he turned to a dripping waiter and took him to task: what did he think of himself, how dare he, and this really was the limit.

Everyone stood around waiting for the fire brigade to arrive. Somewhere in the restaurant a fire must have broken out, otherwise why would the sprinkler system have gone off?

They were all so outraged and busy complaining and swearing wildly that nobody noticed that there was no smoke. It also didn't smell of fire. In fact, nobody had seen even the tiniest flame.

Another thing nobody noticed was the tiny, whirring speck of emerald green that suddenly flitted through the restaurant.

Chapter 2

The green speck whizzed through the sprays of water, first into one corner, then the other. It inspected the entire restaurant. Then the tiny creature flew through the service hatch into the gleaming white and stainless steel kitchen. It was raining here, too, and the water sizzled in the hot pots and pans.

At one end of the kitchen there was an open window. Behind the window was a small, dirty yard full of stinking garbage bins. Like a mini helicopter, the green speck hovered in the air and chirped, 'The coast is clear, you can all come in here!'

A second later, a shaggy grey wolf jumped through the open window and landed skidding uncertainly over the smooth, wet floor. He was immediately overwhelmed by the smells floating in the kitchen.

'Make way!' called a purring but powerful voice. With an elegant leap and without so much as touching the frame, a jet-black panther shot through the window. Her amber-coloured eyes surveyed the strange surroundings. 'Brrr . . . water! I hate water!'

'I thought cats liked being clean,' teased Hamlet, the grey wolf.

A screeching sound made them turn with a start. A baboon with a colourful face was crouched in the window, hopping up and down impatiently and baring its teeth. 'Sheba! Hamlet! You're in the way! Move!'

Hamlet and Sheba, the lady panther, hurriedly moved aside to make room for Ludwig. The monkey jumped nimbly over the tables on which food was being prepared. Then an enormous black mountain of fur and leathery hide appeared at the window. It was so huge that it blocked out the light coming into the kitchen. 'Oh man, Hammy, I don't fit through!' moaned the gorilla.

Hamlet looked up at him. 'Don't worry, Barney. You just need to . . . umm . . . hold your breath!'

Barnabas plonked himself on the window frame. His arms and legs were already in, but the rest of him was still outside. He held his breath, but it didn't make any difference.

'Hard to believe we're supposed to be related,' sniggered Ludwig the baboon and let out a shrieking laugh. 'You fat lump of lard!'

'Bah!' replied Barnabas. 'These are all muscles!' He grasped the window firmly and pulled with all his strength. His face twisted with effort. The window creaked and cracked and suddenly the wooden frame splintered and came off the wall. The gorilla tumbled into the kitchen along with the broken window. Panting, he heaved himself to his feet and picked a few splinters off his shaggy coat. 'See—all muscle!'

Sheba turned away with a shake of her head. 'These primates! Not an ounce of elegance in their bodies . . .'

But then Tulip Blossom, the skunk, scurried up and jumped on Barnabas's furry back. 'Awesome, Barney!' she piped.

'You were awesome, too,' Barney returned the compliment. 'The way you turned on that fire . . . fire whatchamacallit . . . just amazing!'

'Fire alarm,' said Sheba helpfully.

'That's what I meant.'

'It was real easy,' said Tulip. 'The humans never even noticed me—they were so busy. I simply ran through their legs and pressed the red button back there. And right away it started to rain. Rain inside a house! Isn't it crazy, all the things they think up? And then they run away from their own invention.'

'But one thing is crystal clear: the humans will soon be back in here!' twittered Spy, the hummingbird.

'Spy is right,' said Hamlet firmly. 'We haven't come here to have fun! We don't have much time. Let's get started!'

The animals didn't need to be told twice. After all, they had a mission to accomplish: getting food! The little band sprang into action immediately.

Sheba bounded across the wet tiles and found a stack of tablecloths. She spread one on the floor with her paws. Then she leapt up on a table with piles of raw meat and pushed the meat chunks down so that they fell neatly on the cloth. Tulip helped her as best she could.

It was easier for Barnabas and Ludwig. Both monkeys had brought along gigantic sacks that they had found in the streets on the way. They now filled these with fruits, vegetables and whatever else there was.

'Wow! We've really hit the jackpot this time!'

grunted Barnabas excitedly. 'Just look at this stuff, it's absolutely yummy!'

'I've got to say I agree with you,' said Ludwig as he sniffed and nibbled at a small mushroom before tossing it in his sack along with a whole basket of mushrooms. But he turned up his nose at some strange-smelling green fruits that he didn't recognize.

Barnabas was less choosy. He simply shoved everything that lay on the stainless steel tables into the sack with one sweeping movement of his arm. A few bananas fell on the side. Quickly, he stuffed one in his mouth without bothering to peel it. And then another one. And another. And another.

'Barney!' cried Hamlet. The wolf was suddenly behind him. 'You can eat later! We don't have time for that right now! The humans may realize any minute that there isn't really a fire, and then they'll discover us!'

'Sure, sure, Hammy,' chomped Barnabas and hurriedly swallowed the bananas. 'The thing is that the bananas are going to get squished if I take them along, that's why I have to eat them now, see?'

There was no point getting into an argument with Barnabas about food. 'Just hurry up, okay?'

Hamlet, whom the animals had chosen to be the leader of the food-raiding party, was far too excited to help the others. He had to make sure that everything went off without a hitch. He kept running over to the swing doors that led into the restaurant and peering through the gap into the empty room, where it was still raining. Through the large window he could see humans standing on the street, still yelling and gesticulating wildly.

Suddenly, a black-and-white furry something with a bushy tail darted over the tables. The skunk sniffed and licked and nibbled at everything lying on the wet plates.

'Tulip!' said Hamlet in a low voice. 'What are you doing there? The humans will see you!'

'Sorry, Hamlet. I just wanted to taste this stuff!'

'Come back down!'

But Tulip was so fascinated by the many different tastes and smells that she hardly took notice of what the wolf was saying. 'Just a minute, Hamlet. This here smells really divine, let me just quickly . . .'

Hamlet pushed open the swing door and stepped into the restaurant to shoo the skunk from the table.

At that very moment, the sprinkler system switched off and instantly it stopped raining. The sound of water died down and now it just dripped softly from the ceiling.

Some people on the street noticed and peered in through the window.

Quick as a flash, Hamlet darted under a table. The wet tablecloth almost reached to the floor. Carefully, he peeped out from under it. Some people came closer, but no one as yet dared to enter the restaurant.

And then he saw him: the man in the black suit with the dark moustache and piercing stare. Around him stood three girls talking at him insistently.

Hamlet couldn't believe his eyes. It was Zoo Director Mueller with his daughters!

Spy suddenly whirred next to his right ear. 'The rain is done. And so is the fun.'

'Spy! Look outside. Do you see what I see?'

The hummingbird zoomed out from under the tablecloth and flew to the window. A moment later he was back, even more keyed up than he already was. 'But that is Mueller, the animal killer!'

'Of all the . . . Spy, go warn the others! We have to leave right away! We can't take any chances with Mueller!'

In the blink of an eye, Spy had vanished.

'Tulip, where are you?' whispered Hamlet from his hiding place.

'Still on the table,' whimpered the skunk very softly.

'Are you crazy? You have to get down, otherwise they'll see you!'

'They already have!'

Hamlet risked another glance from under the tablecloth. It was true! Some of the humans looking through the window were now staring at Tulip! A little boy clinging to the hand of a grown-up woman was pointing his finger right in her direction. Hamlet could hear the boy's voice loud and clear. 'Look, Mama, there's a cat on the table!' More and more people turned to look. But no one so far had noticed the wolf under the table.

'Cat!' snorted Tulip, outraged. 'He must be off his rocker!'

All of a sudden, a cool breeze swept through the restaurant. Someone had opened the door. Hamlet risked a look. One of the waiters had entered and was looking at Tulip in confusion. 'How did you get in? Aren't you scared at all of water? You really are a strange cat. Hang on . . . you *aren't* a cat! Hey people! You won't believe it, this is a skunk!'

This immediately caused a commotion. Even Mueller stepped closer curiously and was now standing in the doorway. The hairs on Hamlet's neck stood up.

'I guess this is the end,' whimpered Tulip.

'Come on!' yelled Hamlet. 'Move! Now!'

Chapter 3

Hamlet spun around, tensed his muscles and shot out from underneath the table. With all his speed he headed for the swing doors that led into the kitchen. Two, three bounds and he would be there. He got set to jump.

The swing door opened a crack. But in the wrong direction! Barnabas peered cautiously into the room. 'What's happening, Hammy? I thought we wanted to leave—' was all he could say, when Hamlet slammed into the door with full force. He yelped, hit the ground and lay there, dazed.

'Oh man, Hammy, what are you doing?' cried Barnabas in shock and pushed the door fully open. 'All well, old boy? Are you okay? Can you hear me?' Worriedly, he bent over his friend. Then his gaze travelled to the door, and to Zoo Director Mueller, who was staring at him as if he'd seen a ghost. 'Holy gorilla poop!'

Barnabas quickly grabbed Hamlet and disappeared into the kitchen through the swing doors with the wolf under his arm. 'Red alert!' he shouted. 'Drop everything! Mueller is coming!'

Sheba dropped her food bundle on the spot and ran to the broken window. She was the first one out. Directly behind her Ludwig jumped into the yard, shrieking wildly.

Barnabas was next. It had been a tight fit while climbing in. But now, even with the window frame gone, it wasn't easy for him with Hamlet tucked under his arm. Before he knew it, Barnabas was stuck in the opening again.

'Come on, Barnabas, you can do it!' Sheba encouraged him.

'Do something, Barnabas!' whimpered Tulip behind him. 'I can see that dreadful zoo director. He's coming closer! He'll soon be in here!' Tulip tried pushing Barnabas out, but obviously without much success.

Finally, the gorilla plopped out into the yard. Tulip hurriedly followed him and climbed on her friend's broad, furry shoulders.

From her perch she could look through the window

into the kitchen. The door swung open and Mueller stormed in with rapid, pounding steps. There was a dangerous glint in his eyes. 'He's come in!' cried Tulip. 'Go!'

Sheba sprang up on to the gorilla's back and held on fast with her claws. And off they went! Barnabas stretched out his free arm, leapt up and clung to the ledge of a window on the first floor. With ape-like agility, he clambered up the wall of the building at breakneck speed, up towards the sky, with Hamlet under his arm and Sheba and Tulip on his back. Ludwig could climb well enough himself; he didn't need Barnabas's help. The damp and dirty yard receded below them.

Fascinated and fearful at the same time, Tulip looked down. The head of Zoo Director Mueller suddenly appeared in the broken window opening, looking around searchingly. But before he could look up, Barnabas had swung himself over the rain gutter and landed with a crash on the slippery red tiles of the sloping roof. He ran on hastily until he reached the roof ridge at the top. Mueller would not be able to see him here.

Barnabas crouched and caught his breath. Worriedly he cradled Hamlet in his arms. The wolf slowly regained consciousness. His eyes fluttered open.

'What . . . what happened? Zoo Director Mueller! We . . . we have to get away!'

'Shh, lie still,' rumbled Barnabas. 'We've already got away. You were knocked out for a bit. Everything's fine now.'

Hamlet heard the gorilla's warm, comforting voice as if through layers of cotton wool. His head felt numb. But slowly it became better. 'Put me down,' he asked.

Barnabas set his friend down carefully on the ridge

of the roof. Slightly confused, Hamlet looked around. It took him a while to realize where he was: high, high up on a pointed roof. For both monkeys it was no problem to keep their balance. Nor for the little skunk. And a big cat like Sheba practically felt at home here. But wolves weren't as gifted at such dizzying heights. Hamlet's heart began to pound. 'Maybe . . . it's better you hold me after all.'

'No problem, Hammy. I'll carry you back home.'

'Where's Spy?' Tulip suddenly asked.

As if on cue, the tiny, emerald green hummingbird came flying up. He had hidden in an open pot in the kitchen and now reported back to his friends. 'Mueller did see the two of you, but figure it out he couldn't do. First he sees a gorilla there, then the gorilla has disappeared. Mueller's state of mind is bad; he really thinks he's gone quite mad.'

'Serves him right,' growled Hamlet. 'But now we should head back home as fast as we can. Today isn't really our lucky day.'

Together they started on their journey home. Spy searched for a way across the rooftops that the animals would be able to manage without falling down.

And so they ran and jumped over the gaps made by the streets below without being seen by a single human. Finally they reached an abandoned building site that lay in the middle of the city. The place was dense with weeds. Humans dumped their garbage here and sometimes children played nearby. There were also some forgotten, overgrown rail tracks leading below the ground: the entrance to Paradise.

The animals climbed down and disappeared into the secret tunnel.

* * *

Paradise was actually short for 'Paradise Place'. That was the name written on a wooden sign in the middle of the underground hall where the animals lived. It was an abandoned metro station with several entrances and exits. Luminous lichens grew from the walls. Below, there were two ditches with rusted rails. One ditch had caved in at both ends, the other led into the darkness. The humans had built this hall a long time ago, and at some point they had forgotten all about it. It was now the main meeting place for the Wild Pack.

The Wild Pack was a ragtag bunch of animals who had taken refuge here from the humans. Many of the animals had been captured as babies from faraway countries by humans and later abandoned when they became too big. Others were able to escape from their cages. One way or another, they had all managed to land up in Paradise.

Until a short while ago, they had simply stayed here, everyone keeping to themselves. There had been just one rule: no one was allowed to eat anyone else! Then Hamlet, the wolf, had joined them. He had fled from the zoo when Mueller, the zoo director, intended to kill him for his fur coat. Ever since Hamlet had arrived at Paradise, everything had changed. The animals had joined hands to defend their hiding place and prevent it from being discovered by the zoo director. Together, they had freed Hamlet's best friend, Barnabas, from the zoo. And for the first time, they experienced that together they were much stronger than if they fended only for themselves. Together they could achieve so much more.

Earlier, the Wild Pack used to survive on leftover food scraps thrown away by the humans. But all that had changed. They now organized regular food raids. The swiftest and nimblest animals would set off and collect food for all. Five times already they had stolen from restaurants in which the humans ate. Five times they had come back with loads of food, enough for everyone. It had been a little risky, of course, but today was the first time that things had gone wrong.

When Hamlet, Barnabas, Tulip, Sheba and Ludwig entered the hall, the other animals were already waiting for them expectantly. Spy remained outside. He didn't come inside Paradise very often because he preferred being out under the open sky.

'There they are!' exclaimed Oscar and hopped out of the gully where he lived, leaving a trail of water behind as he waddled towards his friends. Oscar was the strangest animal in the Wild Pack. With his duck bill, webbed feet, otter tail and waterproof fur he looked like a mix of all sorts of animals. No one knew what kind of creature he was, and neither did he.

Coca and Too, the two white parrots, fluttered down from their favourite perch on the wooden sign and landed on the dusty concrete floor. Caramba, the ink-blue frog, hopped nearer. Roswitha, the giant tortoise, stretched her wrinkled neck curiously out of her shell. And a grey something that had been squatting on the heating pipes climbed down the vertical wall head first. In the process, it slowly changed its colour from the grey of the pipes to the brick red of the wall. It was Stoplight, the chameleon. 'There you are!' said Stoplight. 'But what's this? I see no piles of food?'

The raiding party came towards them, a dejected lot. One by one the animals jumped out of the ditch. The only one with a little bundle was Ludwig. Barnabas and Sheba had left theirs behind when they had hastily fled.

'Sorry, guys,' said Barnabas squatting down among the other animals. 'This time a lot of things went wrong. First it rained—that was still fine—but then Hamlet banged into the door head-on because Mueller suddenly showed up and the . . .'

'Mueller?' exclaimed Stoplight, taken aback. 'That awful zoo director?'

Barnabas and Hamlet took turns to narrate what had happened. The other animals listened with bated breath.

'. . . and that is why our haul today isn't as big,' concluded Hamlet sadly.

'Still, you've been mighty lucky,' said Oscar. 'Things could have ended up much worse.' Then he approached Ludwig's bundle curiously. 'But what have you brought?'

The baboon screeched and snatched the bundle away. All the animals looked at him, shocked.

'That's not enough for everyone,' he growled.

'That's true,' said Sheba softly. 'All the more reason that we distribute it fairly so that everyone gets at least a little food in their bellies.'

'Why?' snarled Ludwig and clutched the bundle close to himself. 'Why should we share it? This is my food. You dropped yours. Is that my fault?'

'It is *our* food, Ludwig,' intervened Hamlet. 'That's what was agreed from the beginning.'

'Bah! You agreed, not me!'

'All of us set off together, Ludwig: Sheba, Tulip, Barnabas, Spy, you and I. If Sheba had brought along her loot and you had left yours behind, she would surely have shared with you.'

'So? If she's dumb what can I do? Just because Sheba would share doesn't mean I have to do the same!'

'So basically it should be enough for you, is it?'

'Yes! After all it's *my* food!'

'We'll see about that.' Hamlet lowered his head, growled and moved threateningly towards Ludwig. The baboon screeched, protecting the bundle with his body, and bared his scary, pointed teeth.

Chapter 4

A muscular black shadow suddenly jumped between them. 'Stop it!' cried Sheba, looking first at Ludwig, then at Hamlet with her amber eyes.

'But he—' began Hamlet, but was again interrupted by the panther.

'He is right, Hamlet.'

'He's right? How can you say that, Sheba?'

Hamlet was not the only one who was upset. Tulip's tail was raised and had become even bushier. Stoplight's scaly skin started flickering in a range of colours. Coca and Too screeched at Sheba.

All of a sudden, Sheba roared. None of the animals had ever heard her roar like that before. There was a stunned silence. 'You can't force him!' she continued in a velvety but commanding tone. 'No one can force anyone to do anything they don't want to. There is just one rule here: no one eats anyone. Everything else is up to you. Whether you go out to hunt for food or not, whether you want to share it with the others or not—that's something everyone has to decide for themselves.'

'But if you share with the others and Ludwig doesn't, then that's not fair!' interrupted Tulip Blossom.

'That's freedom,' replied Sheba. 'The freedom to do whatever one thinks is right. And freedom is the most precious thing we have.'

'See!' cried Ludwig. 'Sheba is on my side!'

'Not at all,' retorted Sheba and glared at Ludwig. 'I don't think what you're doing is right. But it's for you to decide what to do and what not to do.'

Ludwig gave an irritated screech and jumped off with his bundle of food. He withdrew to the concrete steps that led nowhere and which were actually Sheba's favourite spot. Then he turned his back to the other animals and began unpacking his spoils without so much as a second look.

All the animals thought about Sheba's words.

'Well,' Stoplight finally broke the silence. 'I guess there won't be anything to eat tonight then. I can live with that. I can make do with little food. It's you furry creatures who constantly need to fill up.' He turned around and teetered back to his favourite heating pipe, all the while muttering, 'It's no wonder with the kind of commotion you create . . . This constant running about . . .'

'Without us running about there wouldn't be anything to eat!' Tulip called after him. 'If you slowcoaches went out on a food raid, you'd need a month to get back!' But Tulip was not really mad at Stoplight. She was just bitterly disappointed. And hungry. She plodded back beneath the bench in the middle of Paradise Place and curled up into a black and white fur ball.

'Caramba,' croaked Caramba sadly and hopped away.

The remaining animals slowly dispersed. Sheba moved towards her spot on the steps. Quickly, Ludwig gathered up his spoils and scrambled away.

Only Hamlet, Barnabas and Oscar remained.

'Things really went bust this time, eh, Hammy?' said Barnabas sadly. As if in agreement, his stomach rumbled loudly. 'What are we going to do now?'

'We'll just have to go out again tomorrow,' replied Hamlet. 'I'm still getting chills up my spine from the shock of seeing Mueller. Let's first recover and sleep for a bit.'

'Sleeping is good,' mumbled Barnabas. Then his stomach gave another enormous rumble. 'But I don't know if that'll work on an empty stomach.' He propped his heavy body on his knuckles and tried to feel sleepy.

Oscar had listened to the two friends in silence. Now he looked from one to the other with his black, button-like eyes. 'Can I come along tomorrow?' It wasn't the first time he had asked. 'Please!'

Hamlet lay down and put his head on his front paws to be at the same level as Oscar. 'Oscar, but you know—'

'That I'm too slow, I know. But that's not really true! I'm much faster than Stoplight or Roswitha or Caramba! And in water I'm *even* faster!'

'But when we go on a food raid we run through the city and over roofs, not through water!'

'But that's not my fault!'

'I didn't say that.'

'Maybe I could carry him, Hammy,' suggested Barnabas. 'There's enough place on my back.'

'Yes, exactly! Barnabas could carry me!' Oscar looked at the gorilla hopefully.

'And what if we have to get away quickly? You can't

jump, Oscar. If you had been with us today, you'd have been finished. Mueller would have got you. Come on, why can't you understand that it's just too dangerous!'

Disappointed, Oscar hung his big-beaked head. 'When all of you freed Barnabas from the zoo, I was of no help either. And each time you go out for food, I have to wait here with the others. I'm of no use . . . for anything.'

'But that's not true,' protested Hamlet.

'Oh, really? Then tell me when I've ever been able to do anything. Stoplight held up Mueller with his camouflage colours. Spy can find everything out without being discovered. Coca and Too can transport things through the air. And I? What can I do? I don't even know what kind of animal I am!'

Hamlet didn't know what to say. Those few seconds

of silence were enough. Oscar hung his head and shuffled over the dusty concrete to his gully, hopped inside and vanished into the water.

Hamlet looked at his retreating figure sadly. 'Oh, Barney!' sighed Hamlet. 'We're all so different. Some are big, some small. Some have fur, others have feathers, others scales. Some sleep during the day, others at night, and some sleep almost all the time. Some need a lot to eat, others little. Some want meat, others want leaves. Everyone needs something different. How is this ever going to work?'

Suddenly Barnabas laughed his throaty laugh, which always sounded a bit like thunder.

'What's so funny?'

'You,' answered Barnabas. 'You are funny, Hammy. You worry so much. And actually, you're probably just hungry.'

'For you it's always so easy, Barney.'

'And for you it's always complicated, Hammy. Come on now, let's sleep for a bit. Tomorrow is another day. We'll see what to do then.' Barnabas ruffled the wolf's coat and then curled up into a ball. Hamlet nodded in agreement and closed his eyes.

Chapter 5

Zoo Director Mueller wasn't feeling well at all. He was sitting in his hunting room, in a massive armchair of buffalo hide, his head propped in his hands. His gaze wandered around, over the trophies hanging on the wood-panelled walls. They were the stuffed heads of animals he had shot in Africa, America and everywhere else in the world. All at once, he got the impression that the lion, the jaguar and the polar bear were laughing at him. They were laughing because he was slowly but steadily losing his mind. How else was it possible to explain that today he had seen a wolf and a gorilla in a restaurant?

And not just any wolf or any gorilla! They were *the* wolf and gorilla who had been in his zoo, caged, until just a short while ago. Of that he was quite certain. And now they went to the same restaurant to which he had taken his daughters. Wasn't it absolutely impossible!

There was no doubt about it—he had gone mad. Perhaps he had picked up malaria on one of his trips to Africa and hadn't noticed. And now the jungle fever was eating up his brain. It had to be something like that.

'Hey, are you even listening to me?' screeched a shrill voice in his right ear.

Oh yes, and then there was this as well. Constance, his daughter, was buzzing around his chair like an angry hornet, berating him non-stop. She had been doing this ever since they had got home from the disastrous trip to the restaurant. She screamed and ranted so much that he'd got a headache. He couldn't bear her sneering any longer. 'But of course, my dear,' said Mueller in a fatigued voice.

'I'm telling you for the last time that I want a fur coat! Made of wolf fur! And you have to shoot that wolf for me! Otherwise I'll never speak to you again!' She glared at him for a second, then spun around on her heel, her black hair flying behind her in an arc, and stormed out of the hunting room.

The sudden silence crashed over Mueller like a wave. Things were going from bad to worse. It wasn't enough that animals were disappearing from his zoo one after the other, that there were inexplicable gaps in his memory and that he had started seeing ghosts. No, now even his own daughter was turning against him. His youngest, the apple of his eye, his everything! She would turn her back on him if he didn't do something soon. He couldn't let that happen! But where was he to get a wolf fur from if the only wolf in his zoo had escaped? There was no other wolf in the city!

Mueller was desperate. He had to think of something! With an effort he heaved himself out of his buffalo hide armchair, paced up and down along the trophies and tried to think. But he couldn't clear his thoughts. He constantly got the feeling that the lifeless heads above were watching and taunting him. Finally, he stopped pacing and his gaze swivelled from the polar bear to the elk, from the elephant to the buffalo. All of them seemed to be grinning evilly. 'Stop that!' he shouted, enraged. 'You have nothing to laugh about, you filthy beasts! I call the shots here. I'm the one who shot you, remember? And I will shoot a wolf too, as simple as that!'

Then, out of the blue, an idea hit him. Of course! Why hadn't he thought of that earlier? The answer was, literally, under his nose!

He didn't need a live animal! He just needed the coat. And for that, a dead wolf would do just as well.

* * *

Hamlet couldn't settle down. Whenever he was about to drift off to sleep, his thoughts would return to the food raid that had almost gone horribly wrong, to the fight with Ludwig and to sad Oscar. And he would be wide awake again.

The young wolf cocked his ears to listen to the darkness of Paradise Place. All the other animals were sleeping and each of them made its own sounds in sleep.

Coca and Too rocked gently back and forth and squawked softly from time to time. Stoplight had retreated to his heating pipe that ran along the entire hall and was breathing very quietly. Ludwig was crouched on one of the big, broken lamps hanging from chains on the ceiling and was dozing. The baboon appeared to be dreaming because he would start chattering wildly ever so often. Sheba, on the other hand, was purring loudly on her steps. Added to all these sounds were the loud rumbles from Barney's belly.

'This is what it must sound like at night in the jungle,' thought Hamlet, enjoying the concert. The many animal voices sounded sweet and soothing.

But suddenly there was a new voice that didn't seem to fit in with the others. A sad cooing floated through Paradise. It sounded like a frightened bird.

Something splashed softly, and the cooing became louder and more desperate.

Hamlet's ears perked up alertly. Was someone crying? The wolf peered into the darkness. All of a sudden he was very worried. 'Who is that?' he whispered.

'I'm feeling very hot,' moaned someone in the darkness.

Hamlet thought he recognized the voice. 'Oscar, is that you?'

'Yes,' came the weak reply. 'I'm lying in the water. I'm feeling so hot. The water is nice and cool. But I think it's also *too* cold. I'm freezing.'

Too hot and too cold at the same time? That didn't sound good. It sounded as if Oscar was unwell.

The young wolf quickly ran towards the gully in which Oscar lived. The strange animal really was lying on its back in the water and paddling tiredly with its big, webbed feet. Hamlet immediately noticed that Oscar's scent had changed. He could smell weakness and illness.

'What's happened to you?'

The button eyes gleamed feverishly in the darkness.

'Don't know.'

Then he suddenly sank.

Hamlet got a fright. Quickly, he put his muzzle in the water and was just able to catch hold of Oscar. At that very moment there was a screeching sound from above.

'Help! Hamlet is eating Oscar! Everyone wake up! Help! Help!'

Ludwig, who had observed everything from his lamp, was hopping up and down, pointing furiously with outstretched arms at Hamlet. 'He's broken the rule! Just because he didn't get anything to eat one evening he's already started pouncing on us. We must chase him away! Help!' He swung from one lamp to the other, the chains jangling.

In a trice, all the animals were awake. Bewildered, they looked at Hamlet, standing beside the gully. Caramba, the ink-blue frog, hopped closer curiously. Hamlet drew his muzzle out of the water. Carefully, he placed Oscar at the edge of the gully and licked his fur. 'Oscar is ill,' said Hamlet quietly. 'I was only helping him.'

'He's lying! He wanted to eat him!' screeched Ludwig.

Tulip came bustling up. 'Be quiet, Ludwig. Your accusations are just insufferable. If Hamlet says he was helping Oscar then that's the truth. Hamlet would never harm any of us.'

'Caramba!' croaked Caramba approvingly and hopped away again.

Ludwig was so taken aback that he shut up. Then he hissed, 'But he only spat Oscar out because I caught him.'

Tulip looked at Oscar. The little animal with the duck bill, webbed feet and sleek fur was groaning and whimpering most heart-rendingly. His button eyes were shut and he was shivering. 'Nonsense! Oscar is obviously sick,' said the skunk. 'Hamlet was just helping him.'

Hamlet looked at Tulip gratefully. 'But what do we do with him now?'

In the zoo, the keepers would come with medicine in such cases. But there were no keepers here, and no medicine.

'What's happened to Oscar?' asked Sheba, who had joined them. 'I've never seen an animal become so pathetically ill from one moment to the next!'

'I hope it's not contagious!' shouted Ludwig and quickly moved one lamp further away.

But the others didn't pay him any attention. Stoplight came shuffling up and nudged Oscar. 'He definitely needs warmth,' he announced. 'Come on, Barnabas, take him in your hand. Your fat, furry fingers will be like a nest for Oscar. In any case, he will feel better there than on the cold floor.'

Barnabas was there in one bound. He placed the little animal on his hand. 'Just see how he's shivering, poor thing. He needs medicine or something. Maybe herbs.'

'Is there anyone who knows what to do?' Hamlet looked at Stoplight, who was the wisest of them all, but he shook his head helplessly.

'Does anyone else know how we can help him?' Hamlet called out. But no one had any answer. There was a worried silence. Only Oscar's whimpering could be heard, which was getting worse and worse.

Hamlet growled, 'There's got to be something! There is no illness you can't do something about. What did you all do earlier if someone fell ill?'

Stoplight puffed up his cheeks and slowly became yellow. 'Waited till he was well again.'

'And what if he doesn't get well? We can't just let Oscar die!'

'Maybe it's just a touch of bad water,' said Stoplight, trying to calm Hamlet.

'No, it's something worse,' said Hamlet with certainty. 'You can smell it. Oscar is suffering!'

Again the little animal groaned, as if in great pain. The smell of illness had become more intense.

Suddenly, Hamlet's sensitive nose picked up another scent.

Someone was approaching. Hamlet knew the scent but it was a moment before he remembered who it belonged to. 'We have a visitor,' he said and looked across at the big, old car tyre leaning against the wall.

Behind the tyre was a secret passage. The animals had used it once when they were escaping from Mueller. It led into the labyrinth—a maze of underground tunnels and passages deep underneath the city. The labyrinth was a little creepy, but at the same time it was also exciting and mysterious. One reason was that another animal—a creature that rarely showed itself—lived there in a cave. In fact, Hamlet had seen it only once: Rafina, the giant snake.

One by one the other animals realized who was approaching. Ludwig began shrieking. 'That is Rafina!'

'Rafina?' asked Tulip fearfully. 'But normally she is always in her cave! She never comes here!'

'She's smelled that Oscar is dying!' guessed Ludwig. 'She wants to eat him!'

Chapter 6

The animals of the Wild Pack stared nervously at the tyre. Suddenly, the pointed head of a snake appeared in the middle. A forked tongue flicked from its wide mouth, milky grey eyes peered around as the enormous snake slowly slithered towards Paradise Place. Its powerful body shimmered olive green and black, and looked like it would never end.

The other animals retreated—half fearfully and half respectfully—as Rafina came closer and finally sat up in front of them. Slowly, she looked at the group. Then she began speaking in a warm, sing-song voice. 'What sssoundss are thessse? Thisss terrible whimpering and wailing! It disturbsss my dreamssss!'

Hamlet stepped forward. He too, had respect for Rafina, but no fear. 'That is Oscar. He is ill.'

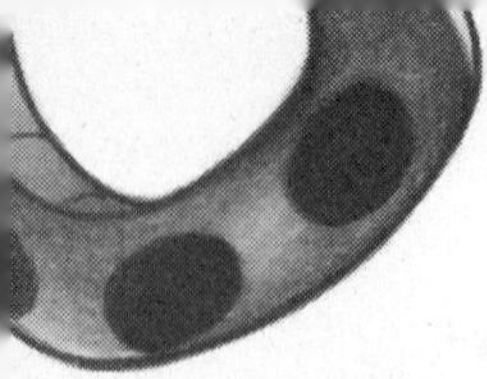

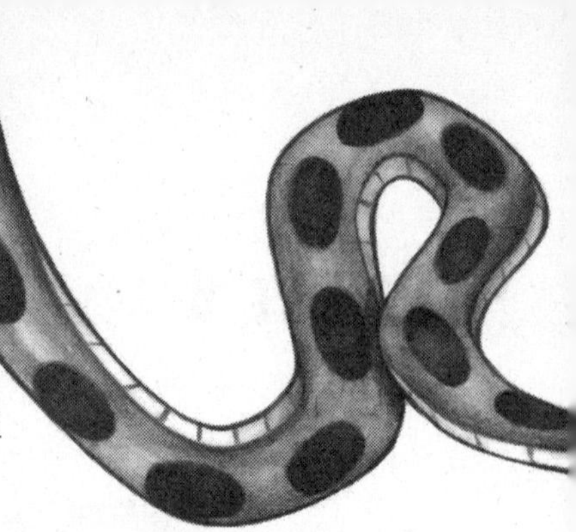

'Let'ss ssseee!' demanded Rafina and slithered forward curiously.

Alarmed, Barnabas retreated and covered little Oscar with his mighty paws. 'You can't eat him!'

'I don't eat sssick animalss.'

Ludwig screeched and swung to and fro on his lamp.

But Barnabas decided to believe the snake and held Oscar towards her. Rafina stiffened and inspected the moaning Oscar for a long time. 'What a sssstrange creature.'

To everyone's surprise, Oscar suddenly opened his little black button eyes. 'Go on, say it,' he whimpered weakly. 'Say that I'm ugly and podgy and useless.'

Rafina seemed to be thinking. 'No. Only ssstrange. Get well, little one. Then I can sssleep again.'

'Do you know how we can help Oscar?' asked Hamlet hopefully. 'Do you know any medicine for him?'

'That he musst know himssself.'

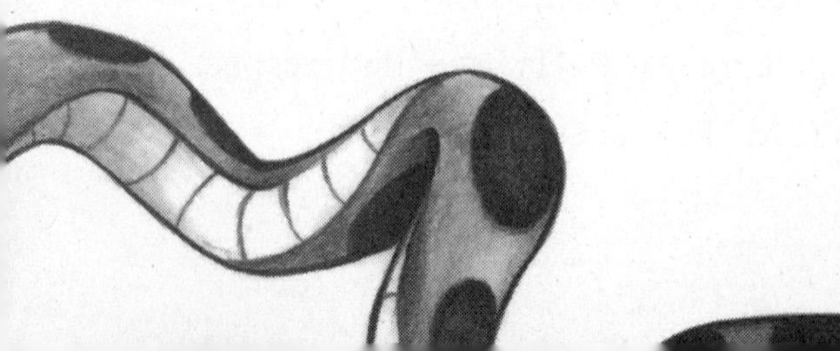

Hamlet couldn't figure out what Rafina meant. 'I don't understand. He should know the cure for his illness?'

'Don't we all?'

'What do you mean?'

Rafina set herself in motion again. Her long body began to coil and the olive-black pattern started to twirl. Before Hamlet's eyes, the black dots began colliding and sliding, above, below and into one another. He felt a little dizzy. 'When you are injured, wolf, you lick your woundss. When you've eaten ssomething rotten, gorilla, you sspit it out until you feel better. When I feel weak, I sssshed my sskin and ssstart anew. We animalss know how to help ourselvesss. That knowledge isss hidden deep inside usss. But sssometimes it gets losst. Like with Osscar.'

'Are you sure, Rafina?' Hamlet persisted. 'Do you really think Oscar knows how he can be cured, and that he's only forgotten?'

The anaconda nodded slowly.

Barnabas turned to the feeble and softly whimpering Oscar. 'Did you hear that, my little friend? You just have to think really hard, then you'll know what's wrong with you. Come on, think hard!'

Rafina hissed softly: 'That isss not going to help. The knowledge isss hidden deep insside him. But he cannot find it again until he knowsss who he isss.'

'Why not?' asked Barnabas.

Sheba came to his aid. The panther had been listening carefully. Now she jumped up and padded on velvet paws between the gathered animals. 'I know what Rafina is talking about. We all have an instinct. That's what makes us different from humans. We sense dangers. We know what is good for us. We know what is bad for us. Which food we can eat and which not to. But sometimes it is difficult. Sometimes we can't do what is in our nature. I would like to sleep on a tree, but there is no tree here. The steps are just a poor substitute.'

'I would like to run,' said Hamlet. 'Under the open sky in clear, cold air. But that is dangerous in the city.'

'And I could just keep climbing,' mumbled Barnabas.

'See?' said Sheba. 'Here in the city we can't do what we actually want to do. We can't be who we really are. For Oscar it must be even more difficult. He doesn't even know what kind of animal he is. Or where he's from. He has lost his instinct. How shall he know what will make him well again?'

Rafina gave a satisfied nod.

'So what can we do?' asked Barnabas helplessly.

'I can transssport myssself back to my home in my dreamsss,' said Rafina and began coiling herself. 'Into an endlesss, lussssh, dark green. Into a heavy, humid warmth. I need my dreamsss of my evergreen home ssso that I don't fall ill.'

'Oscar doesn't have all that,' put in Stoplight. 'He has no memories he can hold on to. He came out of an egg, and no one knows where this egg came from.'

Once again silence fell, interrupted only by Oscar's feverish moans. He was getting worse by the minute. He didn't even open his eyes any longer.

'I think I know what we can do,' squealed Tulip in sudden excitement. 'Once, while hunting for food, I met a marten. And he told me about this special house in the city. It's really big and old and no one lives there, but thousands of humans go there every day. It's called museum.'

'And?' asked Hamlet, who couldn't quite figure out how this would help them.

'The marten told me that the humans collect their knowledge in this house, especially their knowledge about animals.'

'But how can you collect knowledge?' interrupted Barnabas. 'Knowledge is something . . . you know!'

'I'm only telling you what the marten said. But if it's really true, if you can find out things about animals in this house, then maybe we can find out something there about Oscar! And how we can help him!'

Excitedly Tulip scurried between the others. 'What do you think?'

'What utter nonsense!' screeched Ludwig.

'Not at all,' Coca shouted back. 'It's a good idea!'

'I agree,' said Stoplight.

'I don't!'

Everyone began talking excitedly at the same time. Then Rafina's warm, sing-song voice pierced through the chatter: 'Knowledge,' she said mysteriously, 'is sssomething you can never have enough of.'

Hamlet jumped up. 'Tulip, do you know where this house is?'

'In the middle of the city. The marten described it to me. I think I could find it.'

'Then count me in!'

'You want to go to a house of the humans?' screeched Ludwig and jumped to the next lamp. 'How idiotic! They'll catch you and pull your skin off over your ears!' His snout trembled with indignation.

'You don't have to come along,' growled Barnabas. He blew his warm breath over poor Oscar's coat. 'I'll go with Hamlet and Tulip. I want this little one here to get well.'

'If you leave right away, in the middle of the night, there won't be any humans about,' purred Sheba. 'And then a pair of cat eyes might come in handy. I'll come with you.'

Stoplight stepped forward. 'Barnabas, you shaggy rag, would you mind carrying me along with Oscar? If there really is a place where animals can learn more about themselves, I wouldn't mind accompanying you.'

'No problem.' Barnabas lifted Stoplight on to his shoulder. The chameleon slowly took on the dark colour of the gorilla's coat.

'A houssse full of human knowledge,' hissed Rafina and turned around. 'Perhapsss you will ssseee things that you don't want to ssseee.' With that she slithered through the car tyre back into the labyrinth.

Chapter 7

The six of them soon headed off, leaving Paradise Place through one of the tunnels. Outside, it was the dead of the night.

With Barnabas's help, the animals were soon up on the rooftops of the city. Hamlet drew in deep breaths of air, then tilted his head to listen. 'Most of the humans are sleeping, and up here we're safe from those who are not.' He looked across the roofs. Below them, lights were still shining in some houses, and the streets were brightly lit. The constant drone of cars had not stilled even now, in the middle of the night. While the humans might sleep, the city never did. Sometimes it appeared to Hamlet that the city was a living creature itself.

A new sound suddenly became audible amidst the humming of the streets. It was a high-pitched buzzing that only Hamlet heard at first. The young wolf had excellent hearing and could even detect bats squeaking miles away. But what was approaching now was not a bat. It was the rapid beating of tiny wings. Seconds later, Spy whirred in the air in front of Hamlet's nose.

'Why are you all still awake? And on this roof, for heaven's sake?' asked the hummingbird curiously.

The animals took turns telling Spy about Oscar's mysterious illness and their plan to search for the place where they could discover more about him.

'The museum,' explained Tulip. 'We think we may be able to find a cure for him there.'

'I think you're right; your idea is bright,' chirped Spy. 'Humans like to hunt and kill, but also to collect at will. Cups and plates, cars and cash; money in crates they greedily stash. Things living or dead, animals and plants; books to be read, songs to dance. Tables and chairs, socks and shoes; birds and bears, and knowledge, too.'

'We have to get to the centre of the city,' said Tulip. 'Can you show us the way, Spy?'

Eagerly, the tiny hummingbird shot into the air. 'The way is clear. Follow me, don't fear!'

They were just about to set off when a fearsome growling came out of the dark. All of them froze in fright.

'What was that?' snarled Sheba in alarm.

For a few seconds no one answered. Then Barnabas said sheepishly: 'Me. I mean . . . actually my stomach. I'm so hungry!'

Sheba bared her teeth. 'Could you please turn that off?'

The gorilla hung his head. 'I'd need to eat something to do that.'

'Good heavens!' Sheba looked towards Hamlet. 'What are we going to do? With that racket we'll never get anywhere unnoticed.'

'We'll search for something to eat on the way,' Hamlet decided. 'There's no other option. Be on the lookout, but it has to be quick. We only have another two or three hours of darkness before the humans wake up.'

The Wild Pack raced on. Side by side, the friends jumped from one building to the next following the little hummingbird.

'To the stomach rumbling you can soon say goodbye.

Food is in sight, as promised by Spy!' The little hummingbird appeared in front of Hamlet's nose and flitted to the edge of the roof.

Barnabas ran after him. 'Oh Spy, you're the best!' he panted.

Hamlet also peered over the roof to the street below. A truck was parked on the kerb, its engine running. The doors of the truck were open and even before he could see anything Hamlet had smelled it: the truck was filled with food! Two humans were busily carrying boxes of the food into a house.

'In the middle of the night?' wondered Hamlet.

'Some humans work when others sleep,' explained Tulip. 'It's nothing unusual.'

'Fine by me. It's not a fancy restaurant, but it'll do for our hunger pangs.' Hamlet looked down again and observed the unloading of the truck for a while. 'We need a plan. One of us needs to divert the humans somehow, while the others . . .'

Suddenly, a huge black shadow beside him vaulted over the edge of the roof and climbed down at lightning speed. Before Hamlet could even react, Barnabas had already reached the ground. With one bound, the

gorilla jumped in front of the two humans and let out a blood-curdling roar.

The men dropped their boxes in fright and ran away screaming.

Barnabas jumped into the truck and disappeared from Hamlet's view. The wolf could only see how the big vehicle began to heave and shake. A few moments later, Barnabas reappeared, loaded with boxes of food. Hurriedly, he swung onto the roof of the truck and from there to the ledge of a balcony, knocking down a few flower pots in the process. They shattered on the street with a loud bang. Seconds later, Barnabas was back on the roof. He put down the boxes full of bananas, lettuce heads and pieces of meat, pointed to them and said: 'Help yourselves!'

'Barney!' yelled Hamlet, half angry, half amused. 'That was very . . . rash!'

'And totally cool!' added Tulip, hungrily pouncing on a cucumber.

'And absolutely mental!' panted Stoplight, who was still desperately clinging on to Barnabas's furry back. He had gone completely white.

'Oh! I had totally forgotten about you,' said Barnabas, shamefaced.

'Don't you ever do that again, do you hear? You . . . you . . .' Words failed Stoplight—something that rarely happened. '. . . you crazy ape!'

Barnabas chuckled sheepishly. Then he turned to Oscar, whom he had carefully bedded down next to a chimney before jumping.

Soon all the animals were wolfing down the food, stopping only once they were full. Only Oscar didn't want to have anything. He was barely conscious.

'We need to move on,' urged Sheba. 'The little one isn't well at all.'

Barnabas nodded, polished off one last apple and sighed with relief. He patted his tummy and looked at his friends. 'I think the rumbling is over for now.' Carefully, he picked up little Oscar and the band set off again over the rooftops.

After ten minutes, Tulip halted at the edge of a roof. 'Here we are! Down there is the museum!'

Just across from them, on the other side of the street, a magnificent white house loomed in the darkness. Broad stairs led up to a big, heavy wooden door, flanked on the left and right by towering marble columns that held up the canopy over the entrance. Long windows ran all along the building, but they were shut and it was dark behind the panes. There was a second, smaller building next to the main museum and behind it stood a large church. The bell in the church tower rang three times.

Sheba lifted her black muzzle and sniffed. 'Do you smell that?'

Now Hamlet could also make out a distinct scent of animals in the air, familiar but somehow different. 'The smell coming from the museum is like the smell of the zoo,' observed Hamlet uncertainly. 'And yet it's not the same.'

Barnabas also lifted his broad nose. Then he looked at Sheba and Hamlet, shocked. 'If you ask me, it smells like an animal cemetery.'

'A cemetery? What's that?' asked Tulip.

'I can tell you my friend, it'll make your hair stand on end!' cheeped Spy, hovering in the air in front of them. 'When life ends, you lie down and feel cold; your feathered wings you fold. Your last breath is done, and with the wind it's gone. And where many dead rest, you see, what is called a cemetery.'

'A place of death?' cried Hamlet.

Barnabas nodded. 'Yes! That's what I know of the elephants. They all go to die at the same place. After their bodies have been lying in the sun for some days, it smells like it's smelling here now.'

Now Hamlet looked at the museum with very different eyes. 'Do you think we've come to the right place to find help for Oscar?'

'We'll just have to find out,' said Stoplight. He looked at Oscar who was lying with his eyes closed in Barnabas's hand.

'Very well then. But how will we get in? Spy, can you find a way?'

The hummingbird shot off. 'An entry we need. I shall find one with speed.' The tiny green speck vanished into the darkness. The animals didn't have to wait for long, for Spy was back in no time. 'Over the roof there's a way inside. Worry not, I'll be your guide.' With the hummingbird leading the way, they sped from one roof to the next, leaping over the canyons made by the streets below, until they finally landed on the roof of the museum. They gathered around a skylight that was only half shut. Through the opening came the dry scent of animals that they had already smelled on the other side of the street.

Hamlet lifted his snout into the air. For a second he thought he had scented something familiar among all the strange smells. But at that very moment, Barnabas pulled the skylight completely open and a flood of scents went up Hamlet's nose, erasing the faint smell.

Barnabas put his head into the darkness. Startled, he took a step back.

'Hammy, down there!' cried the gorilla, baffled.

'What is down there?'

'Elephants! There are elephants down there! And they aren't dead! They're standing up on their four legs!'

'Elephants?' Sheba shook her head. 'Can't be. That's just nonsense!'

'But just take a look!' Barnabas pointed down.

One by one, the Wild Pack stuck their heads into the opening. Below them was an enormous room, higher than any room Hamlet had ever seen. It was even bigger than Paradise Place! The faint moonlight was just enough to bathe the room in a pale glow. And it was true: right in the middle of the room there were two towering figures standing motionless with their trunks raised.

'Elephants,' whispered Tulip. 'In the flesh! Spy, do you think you can talk to them? Maybe they can help us.'

The hummingbird shot down.

Almost immediately they heard his clear voice. 'I'm from the Wild Pack, my name is Spy. How do you do? Was just passing by. If you'll permit, and by your leave, I'd like to ask a question, please . . .' But suddenly the humming bird gave a startled squeak and fell silent. A few seconds later he came shooting out of the skylight. Agitated, he flitted from one to the other. 'Their legs are planted firmly on the ground. It looks like they with life abound. But it's all just an attempt to cheat; I couldn't hear but one heartbeat!'

'What?' snarled Sheba. 'But how can dead animals stand? If you're dead, you fall down. You don't die standing!'

'We have to go down and take a look!' decided Hamlet. 'Come on, Barney, carry us down!'

Chapter 8

A few moments later, the hulking figure of a gorilla was reflected against the moonlit glass dome, sliding down a marble column with a wolf, a panther and three smaller animals in tow.

'It's a spooky place, I say,' chirped Spy, 'I think I'd rather fly away!' And in the blink of an eye he vanished through the skylight.

Barnabas landed gently and deposited his friends on the ground. Hamlet looked around. They were in the middle of a large hall. The domed ceiling was supported by several broad, gleaming columns. There were doors and hallways and stairs, all leading in different directions. Inside, it was completely silent. Even the constant hum of the city could no longer be heard.

Hamlet took a few steps. His claws clicked loudly on

the gleaming marble floor, the sound echoing spookily from the walls. The place was giving the young wolf the creeps, but for the same reason he also found it somehow thrilling.

The two huge, lifeless elephants were standing nearby. Hamlet stepped towards them and sniffed. They smelled very different from the elephants in the zoo. More like dry leaves than real, living animals.

'Just look at them!' whispered Tulip. 'They look like they could set off at a trot any moment. But they're completely still. Are they dead?'

'Yes, as dead as a tree that's been hit by lightning,' said Sheba darkly. 'The humans must have done something terrible to them.'

Stoplight was teetering slowly along the cold, marble floor and had taken on the shimmering colour of the marble, sprinkled with colourful splotches that kept appearing because of his excitement. 'I don't find it terrible at all. I find it . . . astonishing.'

'Astonishing? Why?'

'The elephants are dead. And at the same time it's like they are alive. The humans have made them immortal. One may think what one likes of the two-legged creatures, but sometimes they manage to do fascinating things, no?'

'In any case, these elephants can't help us,' concluded Hamlet. 'We'll have to go and check for ourselves if we want to find out anything about Oscar. That's why we are here anyway, not for the elephants. Let's explore the rest of the building! But we'd better split up: whoever finds something will call the others. And if there's danger, we'll all meet here. Let's go!'

The Wild Pack split up. Sheba wanted to take Oscar with her. 'You've carried him long enough,' she said to Barnabas and bent to take Oscar gently in her mouth. 'Don't worry, that's how we cats carry our young ones. Nothing will happen to him.' Once she had him safely in her grip, Sheba ran towards the broad staircase and bounded up the steps.

Barnabas chose the big doorway at the other end of the hall. Stoplight slowly moved towards a narrow door on the side, while Tulip darted into a passage in the opposite direction.

Hamlet was left alone in the hall. His right hind leg was trembling with nervousness. He remembered the familiar scent he thought he had smelled on the roof. But now he didn't smell it any longer. Probably his excitement had played tricks on him. Hamlet shook his tail uneasily and growled. Then he gave one last look at the motionless elephants and bounded towards one of the doors that none of the others had chosen. It was high time they found something that would help Oscar!

The room he entered was much smaller than the hall with the elephants. The moonlight didn't reach in here, but there was another source of light. All around Hamlet there were glass cabinets that were faintly lit from within. Behind the glass he could see things that looked vaguely like skull bones or pieces of fur. It was so eerie that Hamlet didn't want to go any closer. Quickly he ran past the cabinets towards the next door, through which a blue-green light shimmered. Somehow, this light was moving!

Hamlet stepped in through the door cautiously. His gaze fell upon a large opening in the wall through which the blue-green flickering glow came. And in this opening . . . Hamlet stood still and drew a sharp breath. He could hardly believe his eyes. In front of him, two magnificent wolves were running over a vast, snow-covered plain. Behind them was a wide, shimmering night sky in which a strange light was blazing. Could these be the Northern Lights, of which one of the older wolves in the zoo had once spoken? Hamlet watched with shining eyes. He took a few steps towards the figures, then his whiskers bristled.

The two wolves were as still as the elephants in the hall. They looked as if they were running over a thick blanket of snow, and their coats gleamed and shone. But they weren't alive and they didn't breathe. Their bodies had been stuffed with something, their eyes were made of glass and their souls had left them long ago.

Hamlet's heart contracted. He was sad to see his brothers like this, but something else made him happy. The landscape surrounding the wolves was beautiful, and it aroused feelings in Hamlet he had never felt. It was as if a dream played before his eyes—a dream that had been buried so deep inside him that he had never noticed it before.

He let his eyes roam over the landscape. It was just as artificial as his stuffed brothers, and yet it was beautiful. Before him lay the wide expanse of a frozen lake. Beyond were snow-covered mountains with a shining moon above. Reeds grew on the lakeshore and the Northern Lights danced in the sky. Hamlet's heart beat faster. This was how his brothers lived! Under a great, wide sky in a distant, cold land. And that was his home too!

An ancient wolf howl arose in Hamlet's throat and pushed its way out. He couldn't hold it back and howled once—loud and wild.

A great longing stirred within him. How he longed to run with his brothers over the snowy steppe and over lakes and forests at night. How he wanted to howl along with them at the moon and the Northern Lights. He wanted to pick up the scent of other animals and discover all the trails and secrets that there must be in the wild.

Hamlet climbed into the artificial landscape, happy about what his eyes could see but also sad that all this had only been recreated by the humans. He lay down next to the two wolves, closed his eyes and dreamt he was running over the lake towards the mountains. In the silvery light of the moon, he could see the wolf pack running towards him. He could even hear the snow crunching under their paws.

But suddenly it no longer sounded like crunching snow; more like the hard sound of steps on a cold, marble floor: human steps.

Hamlet's eyes flew open and he sniffed. There it was again—the mysterious scent that he had smelled on the roof! But it was much stronger now. It had been in the air all this while but he had been so sunk in his dream that he hadn't noticed. Now, however, the scent of greed that hit his nose was so biting that there could no longer be any doubt.

It was the scent of Zoo Director Mueller! The heavy steps on the cold marble floor were his steps, and they were relentlessly coming closer!

Chapter 9

At that very moment, Sheba was standing in front of a cave in which a pair of black leopard cubs was romping about, while their mother lay a few feet away at the edge of a cliff, gazing down. Two more black panthers emerged from a dense, green jungle. Like spirits of the rainforest, they pushed through the hanging vines, twigs and clusters of fern. It took Sheba's breath away. It was the most beautiful sight the panther had ever seen.

'Where am I?' a weak voice beside her suddenly whispered.

Sheba turned her head. Oscar, whom she had placed by the side, was blinking his black eyes, looking around in confusion. 'Oscar, you're awake again!'

'Yes . . . where are we? And where are the others?'

'We are in a museum. It is a big house built by

humans. We thought we might be able to find out something about you here that could help you.'

'About me?' asked Oscar, surprised.

'Yes. Apparently, knowledge is collected here. Knowledge about animals. But I don't understand this place. I'm only seeing animals that are dead, but at the same time, they look completely alive. Just look!' Sheba showed Oscar the wild, green jungle landscape in which her kind lived. 'It's spooky, I know, but it's also beautiful. If only I knew where it is, I'd go there at once!'

'There,' Oscar pointed with his beak at a rectangular sign hanging next to the display cabinet. It had many colourful patches that didn't make any sense to Sheba. One of the patches was highlighted in red.

'What is that?' asked the panther perplexed.

'A map of the world. Those places in red are where panthers like you live.'

Sheba looked at Oscar in astonishment. 'A map of the world? You mean those funny splotches . . . they are supposed to show the world? The whole world?'

'Yes,' replied Oscar. 'You can see that.'

'I don't see it.'

'I do. Look, there's a red button under the map. Just press it!'

Sheba hesitated. 'I don't know . . . what if it makes it rain from the ceiling? That's what happened the last time when Tulip pressed a red button.'

'I don't think so. Red buttons always do different things,' claimed Oscar.

'Very well,' Sheba gave in. She wanted to be nice to Oscar. The panther raised her paw and pressed the button.

Suddenly, a hollow-sounding human voice rang out. It seemed to come from the button. 'The black panther is a lightly built, agile and swift feline predator. Panthers are not a distinct species, as is popularly believed, but black leopards. In slanting light, the typical spotted markings of the leopard are visible on panthers as well. They live in many parts of the world, mainly in Africa, but also in southern Asia, largely in India. Unfortunately, they have been poached for their beautiful coat. Panthers are hunters. They can move almost soundlessly in the wild and run faster than a car driving in the city. At night, they are at a distinct advantage compared to their spotted relatives since they literally melt into the darkness. But even panthers can become prey. They avoid bigger cats, such as lions and tigers, and baboons too, can be dangerous for panthers.' The voice fell silent.

Fascinated, Sheba kept turning her head from the display to the red button to the map of the world to Oscar and back. 'The red button spoke! And he knows something about panthers!'

'Yes!' said Oscar. 'Do you think he also knows something about me?'

Sheba immediately pressed the button again. The information about panthers and leopards was repeated word for word and then the button fell silent again. 'It only knows about panthers,' muttered Oscar, disappointed.

Sheba tore herself away from the jungle scene that aroused such warm and fuzzy feelings in her. They were here to help Oscar! She had almost forgotten that. 'I'm sure we'll also find something about you somewhere here. Come along, little friend. Let's go and search!' She bent to take the little furry animal in her mouth, but Oscar was already moving ahead on his own.

Side by side they ran through the dim light of the museum, past glass cabinets and charts showing different scenes and animals. There were birds sitting motionless on rocks or artificial trees, fish swimming through blue air that looked like water, big-hoofed animals with horns galloping over a seemingly endless, yellow-brown savannah.

'What if I'm not here at all?' asked Oscar suddenly. 'What if the humans know everything about panthers and wolves and about all of you—and nothing about me? Maybe I'm the only one of my sort and just have to accept that.'

Sheba stopped and looked at Oscar. 'You would always have us as friends,' she said warmly. 'Nobody can take that away from you!' Just then, Oscar's eye chanced upon a display and he stood thunderstruck. 'Sheba! Take a look at this wonderful cave!' Oscar hurriedly waddled to the display case, which showed a narrow mud burrow at the edge of a stream, water splashing at its entrance. 'It looks as if it's been made specially for me,' sighed Oscar. 'That's exactly the kind of burrow I would build in my gully if I could.'

'How do you know that?' asked Sheba.

'I don't know how I know,' replied Oscar, 'but this is how I would make it, that's for sure.' Hurriedly he circled the glass case. 'What kind of animal belongs here? Everywhere else there is one.' His eyes suddenly lit up. 'Sheba! Can you see the tracks there? Just in front of the entrance to the cave?'

Sheba craned her neck. 'Yes!' she cried. 'And they look just like yours!'

Excitedly, Oscar wagged his bill. 'Maybe there is an animal just like me in there usually, but now someone has taken it away. Oh, why did it have to be now?' Oscar couldn't bear to only look at the display. 'Can't I crawl in somehow? I just have to put my feet in those tracks. If they fit then I'll know that there are other animals like me!'

They searched for an opening, but the glass case was closed on all sides. Then Sheba discovered something. 'Look, Oscar, another map, or whatever you called it! That big round red patch is down on the right now. There must be caves like this over there. And there is also a red button!' She looked at Oscar inquiringly. 'Shall I?'

Oscar nodded excitedly.

Sheba pushed the button with her snout. Once again a human voice spoke, but this time it told a different story.

* * *

Mueller's steps came closer and closer. Hamlet looked around for a way to escape. But the room had only one door—the one he had come in through. He'd run straight into Mueller if he went out that way!

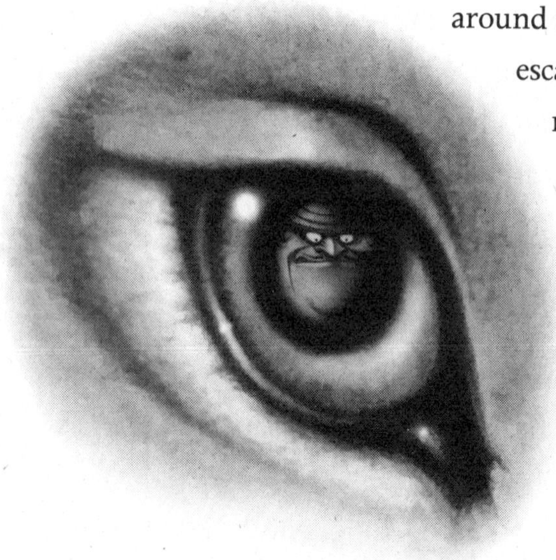

There was only one thing for Hamlet to do: stay put where he was. He held his breath and tried not to move. Mueller was already in the doorway!

Once again, he was wearing his sola topi and khaki-coloured hunting outfit with black boots. His steps echoed loudly as he came towards the display and then stepped on the artificial snow where Hamlet lay. 'Hello, little wolves.'

The voice was icy-cold and power-crazed. Hamlet had to make an effort to stop trembling. He mustn't move now at any cost!

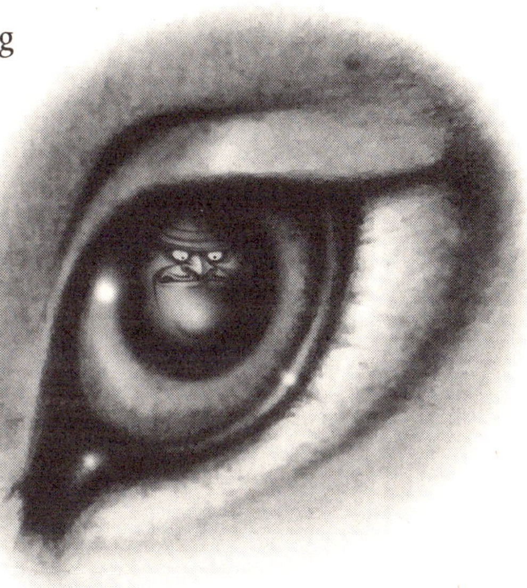

'I was so looking forward to seeing you that a little while ago I even thought I heard one of you howl.' The zoo director stood in the middle of the wolf display as he inspected Hamlet and his lifeless companions with gleaming eyes. He chuckled. 'My imagination must have been playing tricks on me again. But at least my brains are still sharp. I knew I'd find a fur coat here! Constance will get her birthday present after all. Hmm, now which of the three of you should I take? I think . . . this young one looks just right.'

Mueller stretched out his hand towards Hamlet and ran it over his coat. 'Amazing,' he muttered. 'How do these animal stuffers do it? You feel like you're alive, wolf, you're even warm!' Mueller pulled a big knife out of his pocket. 'Wonderful! Constance won't know the difference between this fur and the one from the zoo. Oh, how happy she'll be!'

Mueller lifted the knife—then stepped back with a start. He could see two wolf eyes glowing in the dark. Worse, the stuffed wolf suddenly opened its mouth, showing a pair of mighty teeth!

'No!' groaned Mueller. His head started spinning. 'Please don't let me faint again,' he whispered. 'I am a zoo director! I am superior to these animals! And these here are just stuffed ones!'

But suddenly, the wolf jumped up! With a ferocious growl he leapt at Mueller, knocking him over. The knife fell to the floor with a loud clang.

Mueller was so taken aback that for a minute he couldn't understand what had happened. Bewildered, he gaped after the wolf, who had jumped out of the display with a giant leap and had now disappeared into the depths of the museum howling like a demon.

'No, that's impossible!' Mueller felt the other wolves. 'These are definitely stuffed, so how can the one with the nicest fur have run off?'

Then, suddenly, it dawned on Mueller that this was the same wolf who had escaped from his zoo! Whom he had clearly seen in the restaurant just a few hours ago! He wasn't imagining all this, it was real! The brute was stalking him and had lain in wait for him here in the museum!

Mueller struggled to his feet and cursed his carelessness. He had left his new tranquilizer gun in the car. His old gun had somehow disappeared—another thing he couldn't remember properly. But he had his big hunting knife; that should be enough to hunt down a wolf. Grimly, he surveyed the pointed blade in the artificial glow of the Northern Lights. It was time to go on the hunt.

* * *

While Hamlet raced through the dark corridors and Zoo Director Mueller took up the pursuit, Oscar and Sheba were listening with rapt attention to the voice of the red button.

'Dear visitors!' it said, 'unfortunately, the occupant of this cave has currently been removed for upkeep. As you will hear, it is quite a special animal.'

'Did you hear that?' Oscar whispered nervously. Sheba nodded. The voice continued: 'Early during the Dreamtime, the spirits of the ancestors wanted to build a totem pole. They had to decide which animals would be shown on the totem pole and which would be grouped together. They found a place for each animal, but one animal presented a problem because they didn't know where it belonged: to the land creatures, the water creatures or the birds? So they asked the animals to settle this question amongst themselves. The birds were the first to invite the animal to join them. "You belong to us," they chirped. "You lay eggs and have a bill." "No no," said the land creatures, "you belong to us because you can run across land and have fur like we do." But then the fish chimed in: "You have webbed feet and you swim as well as we do, so you belong to us."'

Oscar could barely keep still with excitement. 'The red button is talking about me,' he whispered over and over again. 'That animal is just like me! I hatched from an egg and I have a bill! I have fur and I can run on land! And I have webbed feet and I swim as well as fish! Sheba, this is my story!'

At that very moment a loud howl rang through the museum, drowning out the voice of the red button. The fast padding of wolf paws on cold stone came closer. Then Hamlet's cry echoed through the corridors: 'Mueller is here! We have to leave!'

Chapter 10

When Hamlet's warning echoed through the museum, his friends were all at different locations.

Tulip Blossom, the skunk, was rolling in a wide, grassy plain and imagining what it would be like to scurry through the grass every day and play catch with the butterflies.

Barnabas was sitting, happily homesick, in a shady mountain cave amidst the artificial chirping of birds, gazing dreamily at faraway mountains whose peaks glowed in the distance. He drummed on his chest lightly with his fists and chewed absent-mindedly on a long vine.

Stoplight was hanging upside down from a tree and darting his tongue into a swarm of artificial flies, which he flicked into his mouth one after the other and then spat out in a wide arc.

Hamlet's call yanked them all out of their daydreams. Quickly they rushed back to the elephant hall.

They all reached at the same time, even Sheba and Oscar.

'Mueller!' panted Hamlet, completely out of breath. 'He's here!'

'Mueller?' cried Sheba. 'But how . . . how did he get here?'

'I don't know. But he's seen me. And he has a knife! We have to get out!'

'That's really tough luck!' grumbled Barnabas. 'I was just starting to really like this museum. I was searching for something about Oscar when I suddenly landed up in a jungle that looked exactly like the one I've come from! You know, it's really been ages since I was home. And here I could remember what it was like really, really well—'

'We found Oscar!' Sheba interrupted him. 'Or rather his story!'

'What?' Barnabas's eyes opened wide.

'Yes,' squeaked Oscar. 'And I don't want to leave just yet! The story wasn't over . . . the voice hasn't yet said what kind of animal I am!'

'Oscar!' cried Tulip, delighted. 'You're looking completely well again!'

'Yes, but I don't want to go! I want to go back to the speaking red button!' The little furry animal seemed quite angry all of a sudden.

'Speaking button?' repeated Stoplight. 'Oh dear, Oscar, I believe you still have high fever! Buttons don't speak!'

'Yes,' retorted Sheba, 'they do!'

'Oscar, Sheba!' cried Hamlet. 'We don't have any time now. Mueller is here! He's dangerous. And he will—'

'I don't care!' bawled Oscar. 'The red button knows more about me! We haven't heard the story to the end! We have to go back!'

'Oscar, we can't do that. We have to leave immediately, otherwise—'

'I don't want to go! I'm staying here!'

Mueller's pounding steps came closer.

'Barney, you have to get us out of here!' decided Hamlet. Barnabas nodded. Without further ado he lifted up Oscar with his mighty paws. Oscar screeched wildly, thrashed and scratched, but of course he didn't have a ghost of a chance against the gorilla.

'We're getting out now!' ordered Hamlet.

Barnabas lifted his head. The open skylight was directly above them but at a height of at least 8 metres! It was absolutely impossible to reach there from the ground, even for a gorilla. He had been able to slide down the marble column, but it was too smooth to climb up.

Sheba and Hamlet noticed the problem at the same time. 'We'll never be able to get up there,' growled the panther.

'Yes, we can,' said Barnabas. He placed Tulip and Stoplight on his shoulders and tucked Hamlet under one of his mighty arms. Going up to the larger of the two elephants, he gently stroked its cold, grey skin. 'Forgive me, my friend,' he whispered. Then with one giant leap he swung on to the back of the jumbo.

At that very moment Zoo Director Mueller entered the hall. His eyes popped almost out of his head as he saw an enormous gorilla on the back of a stuffed elephant with a wolf under his arms and a few smaller animals on his furry back. At the same time, a black panther crouched and then leapt up elegantly.

Wasn't that the gorilla from the zoo? His gorilla? And his wolf? How could this be happening?

Perhaps he had really gone mad? 'Stop!' shouted Mueller and drew his knife. Then he ran towards the group of wild animals.

'He's coming!' cried Stoplight fearfully. He clutched even harder at the gorilla's fur, his colour beginning to turn dark red. 'We have to get out!'

'The skylight is still too high up!' said Barnabas desperately. He kept crouching to jump, but didn't dare.

'Watch out!' snarled Sheba, who suddenly tensed her muscles and ran up Barnabas's back. She pushed off, flying up like a black arrow. Her paws touched the opening but she couldn't hold on anywhere and crashed down.

'Sheba!' howled Hamlet in dismay. But the black cat turned in mid-air and landed elegantly on her four paws without a scratch.

Mueller was very close now. 'I don't know you . . .' he said grinning as he slowly stepped towards Sheba, holding firmly on to his knife. '. . . but your coat is also lovely. In fact, this is even better: wolf, gorilla and panther. I'll simply gift Constance three fur coats!'

Sheba stiffened and snarled furiously, displaying her dagger-sharp teeth. Mueller jerked back slightly, but he felt safe with the knife in his hand. Grinning, he continued to come closer.

Just then a gigantic black shadow dropped down from above, landing between Sheba and Mueller on the marble floor with such a crash that even the stuffed elephants shook. Barnabas put Hamlet down, drummed on his chest and let out a blood-curdling roar.

Mueller went pale and retreated. A furious panther, a furious wolf and a furious gorilla stood before him with bared teeth. Suddenly, Mueller was no longer sure that he could take on all three.

'Leave us alone, Mueller!' shouted Hamlet. 'Now and forever!'

But all Mueller heard was a low growling.

'If we go any closer we'll be within range of his knife,' said Sheba slowly. 'But he won't dare to attack us either. We have to find a second exit and then let's get the heck back to Paradise.'

'Agreed,' growled Hamlet. 'On your marks, get set, go!'

Mueller hadn't yet decided what he should do, when—as if on cue—the three beasts suddenly turned and ran off. It happened so quickly that they were already storming up the broad steps of the hall before the zoo director could move a finger. Three small animals sat on the shoulders of the gorilla. One was a chameleon. It turned its bulging eyes towards him and stuck out a metre-long tongue. Then the animals disappeared from view.

Mueller gasped for air as he stood rooted to the ground. But then, he had an idea.

Barnabas, Hamlet and Sheba ran as fast as they

could, past their silent and stiff brothers and sisters who were standing in enchanting landscapes and slowly gathering dust. How they would have loved to linger here and lose themselves in their dreams! But there was no time for that.

As they ran through the marble passages and columned halls, Oscar once again began to create a ruckus on Barnabas's shoulder.

'You're running in the wrong direction! You have to turn back! The red button is back there! Hey! Is anyone even listening to me?'

'No,' replied Stoplight next to him. 'Our mission was to make you well and we've obviously succeeded. I only want to get away from here now. I just hope there is another way out.'

'There has to be,' said Tulip. 'Look, right in front—there's an emergency exit! Let's try that!'

Barnabas ran towards the door that Tulip pointed to and tore it open.

Behind, lay a narrow, dimly lit staircase. The steps were no longer made of gleaming marble but of grey concrete, and the railings weren't ornately carved wood but cold steel. Sheba raced up first, the others

following. After a few floors, the stairs ended at a white metal door. Sheba jumped at the handle and pressed it down but the door didn't budge.

'It's locked!' snarled the panther.

'Really?' asked Barnabas behind her and tried his luck. He grabbed at the handle and suddenly he had the whole door in his enormous hands. 'Oh,' said Barnabas. A bit embarrassed, he threw the door down the stairwell, where it crashed down with an almighty clatter. Then he stepped through the opening.

They were suddenly under the open sky again. 'We are on a roof!' called Hamlet. It was a different roof from the one they had come in through. Somehow, they had ended up in the building to the side of the museum without noticing. They looked around, relieved not to be locked in any longer. The cold night air blew over their coats and scales.

'We got lucky again,' said Tulip, and scampered down from Barnabas's shoulder. 'Let's get home quickly! I've had enough for today!'

But that was easier said than done. Hamlet and Sheba ran from one edge of the roof to the other, but this side wing of the museum stood apart from the other buildings. There were no neighbouring roofs they could jump on to from here. A house was being built next door and a crane stood on the building site. But the house was not yet ready and was still too low. All the other buildings were too far away. The nearest was a church tower, but even Barnabas would not have been able to reach it, try as he might.

'Now what?' asked the gorilla, stumped.

'We have no choice,' said Sheba. 'We have to go back.'

'Yes!' cried Oscar enthusiastically. 'Back! Let's go back!'

Tulip was already on her way. She had entered the staircase and hopped down the first stairs when suddenly she heard steps. They were unmistakeably Mueller's heavy boots. Fearfully, Tulip peered down the stairwell. There he was! Puffing and panting, the zoo director was slowly coming up the stairs. He was just climbing over the door that Barnabas had torn from its frame. And then Tulip noticed something terrible: Mueller had a gun that was bobbing up and down from his shoulder.

Quickly the skunk ran back. 'Mueller is coming!'

'Never mind,' said Sheba. 'We'll just knock him down.'

'That won't work. He has a gun with him! He must have got it from outside!'

The Wild Pack froze. The staircase was the only way out! They were trapped!

Chapter 11

Hamlet ran across the roof agitatedly. There had to be a way to escape, and he had to find it. But how? The roof was too high for them to jump down to the street. The church was too far away to reach with one leap. And the crane at the building site . . .

An idea struck the young wolf. 'All of you come here!' he called to the others. 'Barney, you first! And the rest of you, hold on to him tight!'

'What's your plan?' asked Tulip hopefully. Hamlet pushed Barnabas to the edge of the roof facing the church. The crane stood exactly midway between the church tower and the museum. Hanging from it and almost level with them was a large, dirty cement bucket, about as big as Barnabas. Barnabas looked in turn from the bucket to the church tower to Hamlet. The gorilla guessed what his friend wanted him to do. 'Oh no, Hammy! You can't be serious!'

'Trust me, Barney! I know you can do it!'

The others hadn't yet caught on to Hamlet's plan. They just hurried to get a firm hold of Barnabas's shaggy coat. Only Sheba was sceptical. 'What is Barnabas supposed to do?'

'No time for explanations, Sheba!' urged Hamlet. 'Get on!'

Barnabas looked at Hamlet. 'Okay, Hammy, if you think I can do it, then I'll believe it too!' The gorilla took a deep breath.

Sheba reluctantly jumped on his shoulders. Barnabas wedged Hamlet under his arm, took a run-up and began racing towards the edge of the roof like a maniac. His friends screamed with fear. Suddenly it was clear to everyone what Barnabas was supposed to do: try and reach the cement bucket hanging from the crane in one jump!

Sheba panicked. She snarled and at the last moment jumped off from Barnabas's shoulder on to the roof. A second later, the gorilla soared over the edge with a giant leap, hooting with joy.

Hamlet, Tulip and Oscar closed their eyes. Stoplight had turned ashen and was screaming: 'Furry creatures are craaaaaaazyyyy!'

The building site slipped away beneath Barnabas's powerful figure, but the gorilla only looked ahead. He flew towards the cement bucket and stretched out his arm, barely managing to catch hold of it with the tips of his fingers. But that was all he needed! With all the strength of a giant ape he pulled himself up and hooked himself to the edge of the bucket. He was now dangling in the air beneath the crane, with his friends in tow.

Barnabas laughed. 'Did it!' he bellowed at the top of his voice. 'I *did* it!'

'But what about Sheba?' cried Hamlet.

'We'll go get her!' promised Barnabas and started swinging. In the cold night breeze, high above the roofs of the city, Barnabas's swinging set the bucket in motion. Oscar clung on for dear life. 'This is like a whirlpool,' he squeaked.

'Whirlpool? You have absolutely no clue,' panted Stoplight. 'This is much worse! I feel like a flying chameleon, and I don't think nature ever planned for there to be any flying chameleons!'

Barnabas giggled. Slowly at first, then with increasing speed they swung like a pendulum between the roof of the museum and the church tower. But shortly before reaching the tower, the bucket swung back. Again they all began to scream. Only Barnabas seemed to be having a whale of a time as they swung towards the roof.

'Sheba!' he shouted. 'Come on, jump now! With you on board we'll manage to reach the church tower!'

The black panther shivered. She wasn't afraid of great heights and she wasn't one to shy away from danger, but to jump on the back of a crazed gorilla dangling from a cement bucket high above a building site just totally went against the grain of a big cat.

At that very moment Mueller stepped on the roof. He looked around searchingly, the gun held ready to fire. But he didn't have cat eyes so he didn't immediately see Sheba in the darkness. Instead, he saw something quite different: a cement bucket swinging back and forth and the gorilla hanging from it.

'This can't be happening!' Mueller stood dumbstruck. But then he grinned. 'A-hunting we will go!' He lifted the gun and took aim at the giant ape.

Suddenly, a snarling creature with amber eyes jumped on him from the dark. Razor-sharp teeth tore the tranquilizer gun from Mueller's hands before the arrow could be fired. Mueller was knocked back and was only able to see his weapon fly over the edge of the roof. 'My gun!' yelled the zoo director, horrified.

Then Mueller's gaze returned to the cement bucket with the gorilla, which was now speeding towards the roof. The other animals were still crouched on the ape. Suddenly, the panther that had just attacked him jumped off the roof, leapt through the air and clung on to the gorilla as well!

Mueller swallowed. 'I don't believe it! There's no

way animals can do that! All this is just a bad dream!' he whispered.

The swinging bucket and the animals vanished from his sight into the darkness.

'Hooray, Sheba!' yelled Hamlet. 'You saved us! And on we go!'

The added momentum provided by Sheba's jump made the Wild Pack swing towards the church tower faster than before. It did the trick, and the bucket hit the tiled roof with a muffled clunk. Barnabas held on to the weather vane and jumped off. In no time, he had climbed down a little way and found an arched window. Lugging the others, he crawled inside the bell tower.

Meanwhile, on the roof of the museum, the zoo director was squinting into the night. Had he dreamt all this up again? The cement bucket he had seen just a minute ago had suddenly been swallowed up by the darkness. On the other side, all he could make out was a church tower. Below was a building site and right in front of Mueller loomed the crane. But where were the animals?

For the second time, Mueller felt he was going to

pass out. Again he had the strange feeling that he was wrapped in cotton wool. Had his whole life turned into a nightmare?

There! In the darkness there was a movement. Mueller leaned over the parapet. Wasn't there something moving towards him? Something big and round? There it was again, the cement bucket! Or wasn't it? Because there were no animals . . . and obviously that was impossible.

Mueller was firmly convinced his senses were playing tricks on him. But that didn't bother the cement bucket in the least. With a loud 'boing', it hit Mueller on the head. As the zoo director keeled over, he saw some stars. And then nothing.

Chapter 12

'We made it!' cried Sheba, half elated, half stunned. 'That was unbelievable, Barnabas!'

'Thank you,' said the gorilla bashfully.

Suddenly Spy was back with them. The tiny, emerald green bird swooped through the dark and alighted on the stone window sill. 'Everything I saw; I was watching in awe! The way you flew, you'd beat me too!'

'Oh no, we're a long way from flying like you!' laughed Tulip.

'Flying!' remarked Stoplight scornfully. 'Flying and running and jumping and chasing all over the place! Can't you feathered and furry creatures move at a normal speed? Could you? Just once? For me?'

Hamlet, Barnabas, Sheba, Tulip, Spy and Oscar looked at each other. 'Never!' all of them said at the same time. And Spy added—'That wouldn't be clever.'

They all burst out laughing again. Stoplight turned his back on them, but his friendly green colouring showed he wasn't really offended. He was just as happy about the successful escape as the others. 'Well, fine then,' he finally said. 'So how about you show what you can do. Let's disappear from this place as fast as we can!'

They decided it would be best to get to the street through the church and climb the next house from there. Barnabas had landed somewhere in the middle of the bell tower. There was a steep, spiral staircase leading down.

'I say it with regret, but these walls make me fret,' chirped Spy and turned towards the window. 'In the garden below, I'll wait—don't be slow! Don't dawdle, be fast; the night will not last!' He lifted off into the air and whizzed out of the tower.

'Spy is absolutely right,' said Hamlet. 'We must get back to Paradise before the sun rises.'

The animals climbed down the stone staircase. It was narrow and dark, and the stairs wound round and round.

'I think we might have enough time to go back to the red button,' Oscar said, his voice echoing strangely in the tower.

'Oscar!' Hamlet turned around. 'I promise that we will go back to the museum. But only when it's absolutely safe! Until then you'll have to be satisfied with what you've learnt so far.'

'Which is quite a bit,' added Sheba. 'And maybe now you can explain that world map business to me because I didn't quite understand.'

'Oh that,' mumbled Oscar and hopped down the next step. 'That's pretty simple. The earth is like this giant ball on which there is land and water. The land parts are called continents and the humans have named them all. Then they've drawn everything on paper in such a way that you can see the whole earth in one go. That's what they call a world map. You come from one of these land parts—and I from another.'

Suddenly he laughed happily. 'I come from a continent! I even know where it is! Isn't that great?' The little animal squeaked cheerily and skipped down the next steps in big hops.

The other animals looked at each other. They were happy and relieved that Oscar had recovered completely.

'If someone knows so much,' mumbled Barnabas, 'he shouldn't think he's useless!'

'Typical of you furries,' grunted Stoplight. 'Thinking has never been your strong point.'

Finally, they reached the bottom of the stairs. An ancient wooden door led directly into the church. One by one they entered the enormous hall and gaped. Luckily, it was deserted. The church was a bit like the museum, but it was also completely different. Everything was made of cold, smooth stone and the ceiling was supported by pillars. The walls gave off the scent of many centuries. The church was even more gigantic than the museum—three elephant halls could have fitted in easily.

'Just look!' whispered Oscar in awe. 'They don't have stuffed animals in here . . . they have stuffed humans!' He pointed towards figures standing in niches all along the wall: rigid human figures with their heads turned to the sky, holding little children or long wooden sticks in their hands.

'They aren't stuffed,' said Stoplight, amused. 'They are made of wood or stone. They are saints.'

'Saints?' asked Tulip. 'What's that?'

'No idea. I heard about them on radio once during the time I was in my terrarium.'

The animals swarmed out curiously, running between the long rows of wooden benches to take a look. Only Hamlet was uneasy. 'We shouldn't push our luck. We should be getting on our way! Spy is also waiting for us.'

Just then Oscar called again. 'Hey! Take a look at this!'

The animals came towards him curiously. Oscar was standing under a row of high, colourful windows. When they looked more closely, they discovered that the windows weren't just coloured, they had proper pictures painted on them.

While the animals were trying to figure out the paintings, the sun suddenly rose, its golden rays streaming through the coloured glass and bathing the church in a warm glow. The sun cast the colours of the glass panes on the floor, just at the spot where Oscar was standing.

The rainbow of beams made the little animal look like Stoplight when he changed colours: red, blue, yellow and dark green shadows gleamed on his coat. But Oscar wasn't looking at the floor; he was looking up at the radiant window paintings. 'Look, it's actually a story!' he cried, delighted.

'What does he mean?' asked Sheba.

Hamlet shrugged his shoulders. He studied the church windows. There was one of a man with a white beard and other humans too. One picture showed a ship that wasn't fully built. In the next picture it was finished, and . . . what was that? Lots and lots of animals! Lions, elephants, giraffes, and at the back, wasn't that a wolf? All the animals went in one by one into the ship. 'Well I'll be . . .' said Hamlet, astonished. 'Do you see that? The animals there?'

'Yes,' replied Sheba. 'I see them. They remind me a little of us. But what were you saying about a story, Oscar?'

'That one there, of course!'

'But those are just pictures.'

'Yes, but humans use such pictures to tell stories.

They draw something that happens in one picture, and in the next picture they draw what happens next.'

Now all of them tried hard to find a story in the pictures. But try as Hamlet, Sheba, Stoplight, Tulip and Barnabas might, for them they remained just coloured glass windows.

'I don't see anything. Can't you tell us the story, Oscar?' asked Barnabas. 'You know, the one of the animals and the ship—it looks kind of interesting to me.'

'To me, too!' said Stoplight.

'Of course,' said Oscar, flattered. 'Right, so in the first picture you see that guy with the white beard. He's looking pretty mad with the others. I think he's probably the boss man and the others are scared of him. They're actually cowering before him. Can you see?'

'Why is he mad?' Stoplight wanted to know.

'No idea.'

'I see . . .'

'In the second picture, he's talking to that family there,' continued Oscar. 'He orders them to do something, and what that is you can see in the third picture: they are supposed to build a ship. And surprise! Surprise! It's a ship for animals! The land in which the humans and the animals lived wasn't so great—you can see that from the dried plants and the broken houses in the pictures. So the guy with the beard probably thought it would be better if the animals could live somewhere else. After all, it wasn't their fault that the plants had dried up. That probably happened because of the humans, so they should jolly well build the animals a ship.'

'And you can see all of that in the pictures?' marvelled Sheba.

'Well, more or less,' mumbled Oscar, a little embarrassed. 'Of course, you also have to imagine a few things.'

'Go on!' demanded Stoplight.

'At any rate, the bearded guy told this family: build a ship for the animals and take them to a land that is better than this one. Then we can be friends again. So the family did as they were told. You see that in the next picture. They build a huuuuuumongous ship. And then all the animals came—tigers and bears and monkeys and ducks and . . .' Oscar narrowed his eyes and peered at the picture. 'I'm not there, unfortunately. Well, never mind! The animals climbed into the ship and put out to sea. They went on a lovely cruise, and the man and his family had to take care of the animals and bring them food and all that. That was probably part of the deal they had with the grandpa.'

'See?' rumbled Barnabas. 'They are just like we are! All of them together in a boat and they didn't eat each other! How does the story go on, Oscar?'

'One day, suddenly, there was a terrible storm. Do you see?'

All the animals nodded solemnly as they studied the picture with the storm. It showed the ship being tossed by mighty waves, and the sky overhead almost black and streaked by lightning.

'But that wasn't so bad because it was a good ship and it could withstand the high waves.' Oscar looked at the last two pictures. 'At some point, the weather got better—there was even a beautiful rainbow. Then the ship reached a large island. The animals sent a white bird to check out this island. The bird looked around, thought the island was great and reported back to the others. Then the animals decided to leave the ship and to stay on the beautiful island. The human family also came along. And together they all lived happily ever after.' Oscar looked at his friends with shining eyes. 'Isn't that a fantastic story?'

'Yes!' cried Hamlet. 'These animals lived in an ugly place and then they got together and travelled to a beautiful land, even though they were all so different. Do you get it? Just like us! These are our ancestors!'

Barnabas scratched his enormous skull. 'But Oscar just said that we all come from different parts of the world.'

'The story with the ship probably happened a long, long time ago,' explained Oscar. 'After that, the animals spread across the entire world.'

Hamlet's yellow-green wolf eyes lit up. 'You know

what I think?' The wolf jumped up and ran through the dazzling shadows that the windows cast over the animals on the floor. 'All these continents that we come from, they are all surrounded by water.'

'By the seas!' cried Tulip.

'Exactly! And if that's so, then if we had such a ship we could sail over the seas and each of us could go wherever we are happiest . . . where there are other animals like us . . . where we belong!' Hamlet spluttered excitedly.

'Other animals like me!' squealed Oscar, overcome with emotion. 'What a brilliant idea!'

'Yes, and you know what the best part is?' continued Hamlet excitedly. 'It would even work because it's already worked once! The animals in Oscar's story simply left the land in which they didn't want to live any longer. What do you think—should we do the same? All of us together! We'll sail over the seas to wherever each of us is at home!'

A deep silence fell over the church.

Then Barnabas whispered: 'A ship! A ship into the jungle!'

'And everywhere else!' yelled Oscar.

'Where one can stick out one's tongue and catch flies,' sighed Stoplight.

'Where I can scamper over a meadow and dance with butterflies!' whooped Tulip Blossom.

'Where other panthers live!' said Sheba.

'Yes, a ship!' cried Hamlet. 'We'll leave the city and travel to a place where we won't have to hide from the humans any longer. Where Mueller can't follow us. That's the answer!' He looked at his friends. 'Are we all in?'

Stoplight, Tulip, Sheba, Barnabas and Oscar thought for a few seconds, then with one voice they all shouted: *'Yes!'*

Chapter 13

On the roof of the museum, Zoo Director Mueller struggled to his feet. He scratched his head in confusion. Why was it so cold? Why did he have such a headache? Why wasn't he in his bed? In fact, where was he?

Mueller looked around. Quite obviously on a roof. But why? He looked more carefully. He could see a dirty cement bucket dangling from a crane in front of him. On the other side was an old church. Behind him, Mueller could see a doorway without a door. What had happened here? Mueller swallowed.

All of a sudden, several strange images shot through his head: images of a swinging ape and of a chameleon sticking its tongue out at him, images of his gun toppling down . . .

Mueller gasped for air. It suddenly dawned on the zoo director that the fur coat for Constance had got away from him! For the second time, if his memory served him right. Mueller was suddenly quite sure that his memory of being in a snake's stranglehold in an underground cave wasn't just a feverish dream. Just like that swinging ape! Hadn't he once owned two tranquilizer guns? And hadn't both vanished?

Mueller bent over the parapet. Down below was the proof, or rather what was left of it. His wonderful new gun lay in the grey mass of a cement mixer, all bent and broken. He could write that one off.

Wearily, Mueller turned around. He remembered everything now: the stuffed wolf that wasn't stuffed, and the animals that had tricked him! But he wouldn't let that happen again. Mueller still had something up his sleeve: a gift he had once got from a big game hunter. He needed to get to it now. He had to leave the museum at once and get home before the first visitors arrived.

When the crumpled zoo director entered his hunting room an hour later, he was smiling grimly. He walked to a glass cabinet standing against the wall in which he kept his hunting guns. He opened it and pressed a small, almost invisible button. A long, narrow secret drawer slid out from the back of the cabinet. In it lay a walking stick. Mueller lifted it out reverently.

The walking stick was smooth and dark, and the silver handle was in the shape of a dachshund head. Of course, it wasn't an ordinary walking stick. Mueller carefully removed the tip, revealing the barrel of a gun. He pressed on a hidden mechanism and a flap in the stick sprung open. Quickly, he shoved two tranquilizer darts into the opening. Finally, he pulled off the dachshund head. The trigger was hidden underneath. What appeared to be Mueller's walking stick was actually a very well-disguised tranquilizer gun—the only one of its kind in the world.

The zoo director smiled as he stroked the black wood. 'This weapon . . .' he murmured, 'I can take with me wherever I go. Nobody will suspect what it is and I'll always have it beside me. Our next encounter, little wolf, is sure to come!'

The smile faded from Mueller's face when furious steps suddenly sounded in the corridor. His youngest daughter stormed into the room. 'Papa!' she shouted in a shrill voice. 'There you are at last! But where is the fur coat? You said I would get it by this morning!'

Mueller winced. He quickly put the tip of the stick and the dachshund head back in place. Then he turned to face Constance. Her eyes glinted with anger and her pitch-black hair stuck out furiously in all directions.

'Constance, my precious,' Mueller said in a pained voice. 'Don't worry! I'll soon shoot that wolf for you. It will be the most beautiful fur coat in the entire world.'

'But my birthday was yesterday!' shrieked Constance. 'And instead of hugging my shoulders, my coat is still at large somewhere!'

Mueller patted her head reassuringly. 'Not for long,' he said quietly. 'Soon you'll have the best fur coat ever, I promise!'

Constance shook her head. 'But you've been promising that all the time!'

'And I will keep my promise.' Mueller looked at his daughter sternly. 'Now, I have to get to work and you to school.' He pushed Constance out of the door and then set off himself. In his right hand he gripped his new stick. It felt good. Mueller took two steps then set the stick down. It touched the ground with a quiet click. Two steps—a click, two steps—a click.

'Your days are numbered, little wolf,' he thought. 'The countdown has begun!'

Two steps—a click.

* * *

When the Wild Pack finally reached Paradise, the other animals were waiting impatiently for their friends to arrive. Even Spy had come along because Hamlet had told him that he wanted to make an announcement to all the animals together. The hummingbird didn't like confined spaces but he was too curious to say no.

'Where were you? It's already day! We thought something might have happened to you!' said Coca and Too.

'So who cares,' muttered Ludwig, the baboon, swinging on one of the old lamps.

Hamlet didn't pay him any attention. 'Listen, all of you! We've discovered something of utmost importance for all of us!'

'What's of utmost importance is whether you've brought along something to eat or not!' screeched Ludwig.

'No, this is much, much, much more important!' squeaked Oscar. He scrambled down from Barnabas's back and slid into his gully, sighing blissfully at being back in the cool water. 'Yes, it's something really wonderful!'

Roswitha, the giant tortoise, and both the goats, who never said anything, came closer curiously. The ink-blue frog looked at Oscar. 'Caramba?' he asked.

Stoplight giggled. 'Yes, Oscar is well again,' he explained. 'And what's more, it turns out he has a quite a remarkable talent that none of us knew about.'

Oscar wiggled bashfully in the water.

'Really?' asked Ludwig sceptically. 'What on earth can he do?'

'He can read pictures,' replied Stoplight, who was quite proud of his friend. 'And maps! And he discovered a fascinating story. Come on, Oscar, tell the others!'

'All right,' said Oscar as he crawled out of the water and shook himself dry. Then he told the other animals the entire story once again: of the ship and the animals and the faraway land.

'Besides, we know now that each one of us comes from a particular continent where we would feel the happiest—our home!' continued Sheba. 'And we can go there in a ship!'

Coca and Too looked at Stoplight and clattered their beaks. Roswitha forgot to chew on the limp lettuce leaf that she had been nibbling on for the last two days.

'And that's exactly what we intend to do!' burst out Hamlet, who couldn't contain himself. 'No more humans! No more Mueller! We will finally go where we belong!'

'Stuff and nonsense!' bleated Ludwig, but nobody paid him any attention.

Barnabas suddenly groaned. 'Oh man, Hammy! We're really daft! We forgot something!'

Hamlet looked at him, irritated. 'What?'

'I mean, we don't have a ship! In the story, the humans built it for the animals. Not willingly, of course! But the guy with the beard ordered them to. But who is going to build a ship for us? Mueller? I don't think he'd do it. And we don't even have someone like the guy with the beard on our side.'

The excited fluttering and scurrying and shouting died down. Only Ludwig laughed. 'I knew it. What a hare-brained plan.'

'Rubbish,' growled Hamlet firmly. 'The humans aren't going to build us a ship, you're right about that, Barney. But we don't need humans for that—we can do it ourselves!'

'Build it ourselves?' Ludwig began screeching again. 'How crazy can you get? Animals don't build ships! Only humans can do that!'

'Then we'll just have to learn,' declared Hamlet calmly.

'Exactly!' Oscar lifted his bill up in the air.

'An animal that can lay eggs, swim, run and dive will surely be able to build a ship!'

Coca and Too giggled. 'You're feeling quite well again, eh, Oscar?!'

A little, green speck buzzed about in the air. 'We have a dream that's as big as a tree, from which we shall build a ship, you'll see!'

'Exactly!' exclaimed Tulip, and wagged her bushy tail in the air.

'We will go where we are free. All together, you and me!' cheered Spy.

'When do we start?' Tulip's question caused the Wild Pack to quieten down again.

Suddenly, all the animals looked at Hamlet. Spy settled on his left ear like a fiery green spark and waited expectantly for an answer. Stoplight's skin glittered and flickered in all the colours of the rainbow. Roswitha had still not resumed chewing.

The young wolf sat between his friends and pondered. Then he looked across at Barnabas, who was watching him with his mouth open, and Hamlet couldn't help laughing. He let out a wild howl that resounded through Paradise: 'Now! When else?'